# Saints in Sonnets

Canon John Kimball Saville, D.D.

CATHEDRAL CENTER PRESS

*Publishers*

ON THE COVER; ST. SEBASTIAN
ISBN 0-9716255-2-2

Cathedral Center Press is an imprint of the Episcopal Diocese of Los Angeles

*To Nellie Anne Daniels Saville,*
*my fiancée, wife and life for 70 years.*
*In her soul lives the love of these dear ones.*

# CONTENTS

FOREWORD    XIII

ACKNOWLEDGEMENTS   XV

INTRODUCTION    XVII

*God The Father*   *3*

*Jesus Christ*   *4*

*The Holy Spirit*   *5*


NOVEMBER

*All Saints*   *6*

*All Faithful Departed*   *7*

*Richard Hooker*   *8*

*Willibrord*   *9*

*Leo the Great*   *10*

*Martin*   *11*

*Charles Simeon*   *12*

*Samuel Seabury*   *13*

*Margaret*   *14*

*Hugh*   *15*

*Hilda*   *16*

*Elizabeth*   *17*

*Edmund*   *18*

*Clement, Bishop of Rome*   *19*

*James Otis Sargent Huntington*   *20*

*Kamehameha & Emma*   *21*

*St. Andrew*   *22*


DECEMBER

*Nicholas Ferrar*   *23*

*Channing Moore Williams*   *24*

*John of Damascus*   *25*

*Clement of Alexandria*   *26*

*Nicholas*   *27*

*Ambrose*   *28*

Contents

*Lucy*   29
*St. Thomas*   30
*St. Stephen*   31
*St. John*   32
*The Holy Innocents*   33
*Thomas Becket*   34

JANUARY

*Holy Name*   35
*Julia Chester Emery*   36
*William Laud*   37
*Aelred*   38
*Hilary*   39
*Antony*   40
*Confession of St. Peter*   41
*Wulfstan*   42
*Sebastian*   43
*Fabian*   44
*Agnes*   45
*Vincent*   46
*Phillips Brooks*   47
*Conversion of St. Paul*   48
*Timothy & Titus*   49
*John Chrysostom*   50
*Thomas Aquinas*   51

FEBRUARY

*Brigid*   52
*The Presentation*   53
*Anskar*   54
*Cornelius*   55
*The Martyrs of Japan*   56
*Absolom Jones*   57
*Cyril & Methodius*   58
*Thomas Bray*   59
*Martin Luther*   60
*Polycarp*   61

*St. Matthias    62*
*George Herbert    63*

MARCH

*David    64*
*Chad    65*
*John & Charles Wesley    66*
*Perpetua & her Companions    67*
*Gregory of Nyssa    68*
*Gregory the Great    69*
*Patrick    70*
*Cyril    71*
*St. Joseph    72*
*Cuthbert    73*
*Thomas Ken    74*
*James De Koven    75*
*Gregory, The Illuminator    76*
*The Annunciation    77*
*Charles Henry Brent    78*
*John Keble    79*
*John Donne    80*

APRIL

*Frederick Dennison Maurice    81*
*James Lloyd Breck    82*
*Richard of Chichester    83*
*Martin Luther King, Jr.    84*
*William Augustus Muhlenberg    85*
*Dietrich Bonhoeffer    86*
*William Law    87*
*George Augustus Selwyn    88*
*Alphege    89*
*Anselm    90*
*St. George    91*
*St. Mark    92*
*Catherine of Siena    93*

Contents

MAY

St. Philip and St. James    94
Athanasius    95
Monnica    96
Dame Julian of Norwich    97
Gregory of Nazianzus    98
Dunstan    99
Alcuin    100
Jackson Kemper    101
Bede, the Venerable    102
Augustine    103
The Visitation    104

JUNE

Justin    105
The Martyrs of Lyons    106
The Martyrs of Uganda    107
The First Book of Common Prayer    108
Boniface    109
Columba    110
Ephrem of Edessa    111
St. Barnabas    112
Enmegahbowh    113
Basil the Great    114
Evelyn Underhill    115
Joseph Butler    116
Bernard Mizeki    117
Alban    118
Nativity of John the Baptist    119
Irenaeus    120
St. Peter & St. Paul    121

JULY

Independence Day    122
Benedict of Nursia    123
William White    124
Macrina    125

*Contents*

  *Elizabeth Cady Stanton 126*
  *Amelia Jenks Bloomer 127*
  *Isabella (Sojourner Truth) 128*
  *Harriet Ross Tubman 129*
  *St. Mary Magdalene 130*
  *Thomas á Kempis 131*
  *St. James 132*
  *Anne and Joachim 133*
  *William Reed Huntington 134*
  *Mary and Martha of Bethany 135*
  *William Wilberforce 136*
  *Ignatius of Loyola 137*

AUGUST
  *Joseph of Arimathaea 138*
  *Oswald 139*
  *The Transfiguration 140*
  *John Mason Nealev 141*
  *Dominic 142*
  *Laurence 143*
  *Clare of Assisi 144*
  *Florence Nightingale 145*
  *Jeremy Taylor 146*
  *Jonathan Myrick Daniels 147*
  *St. Mary the Virgin 148*
  *William Porcher Dubose 149*
  *Bernard Abbot of Clairvaux 150*
  *St. Bartholomew 151*
  *Louis, King of France 152*
  *Thomas Gallaudet &*
     *Henry Winter Syle 153*
  *Augustine of Hippo 154*
  *Aidan 155*

SEPTEMBER
  *David Pendleton Oakerhater 156*
  *The Martyrs of New Guinea 157*

*Paul Jones    158*
*Constance and her Companions    159*
*Alexander Crummell    160*
*John Henry Hobart    161*
*Cyprian    162*
*Holy Cross Day    163*
*Ninian    164*
*Hildegard    165*
*Edward Bouverie Pusey    166*
*Theodore of Tarsus    167*
*John Coleridge Patteson    168*
*St. Matthew    169*
*Sergius    170*
*Lancelot Andrewes    171*
*St. Michael and All Angels    172*
*Jerome    173*

OCTOBER

*Remigius    174*
*Francis of Assisi    175*
*William Tyndale    176*
*Robert Grosseteste    177*
*Philip, Deacon and Evangelist    178*
*Edward the Confessor    179*
*Samuel Isaac Joseph Schereschewsky    180*
*Teresa of Avila    181*
*Hugh Latimer & Nicholas Ridley    182*
*Thomas Cranmer    183*
*Ignatius of Antioch    184*
*St. Luke    185*
*Henry Martyn    186*
*St. James of Jerusalem    187*
*Alfred the Great    188*
*St. Simon & St. Jude    189*
*James Hannington    190*

*Contents*

SEASONS & HOLY DAYS    191
    *Advent    192*
    *Christmas    193*
    *Epiphany    194*
    *Lent    195*
    *Palm Sunday    196*
    *Maundy Thursday    197*
    *Good Friday, The Trial    198*
    *Good Friday, The Crucifixion    199*
    *Holy Saturday    200*
    *Easter Day    201*
    *Ascension    202*
    *Pentecost    203*
    *Thanksgiving    204*

EPILOGUE    *205*

SONNET    *John Kimball Saville, Jr    211*

BIBLIOGRAPHY    *213*

INDEX    *215*

# FOREWORD

In London this past week, I visited the chapel where Archbishop Thomas Cranmer wrote parts of the original Book of Common Prayer, a poetic expression of faith and courage that did so much to build the Anglican Church.

Cranmer is only one of the martyrs, priests, prophets, missionaries, social workers, writers, soldiers and ordinary people listed in the Episcopal Church's calendar of commemorations. None of these people set out to be saints. In fact, like most of us, they were probably just trying to get from day to day. But each of them was willing, by faith in Jesus Christ, to do the work God gave them to do. Each of them serves as an example of how God can use our gifts to serve him and each other.

The sonnets in this book, which celebrate these saints and their enormous contributions to our lives, were created by one of our own living saints, Canon J. Kimball Saville, whose wisdom, kindness, knowledge and hard work have enlightened so many in our diocese. Canon Saville has translated his immense knowledge about these people of God, their lives and their ministries, into verses that take us deep into what it means to be among the saints. It's a delight and an irony that he himself embodies so many of the characteristics that he celebrates in these poems.

The great hymn for All Saints' Day, Sine Nomine, says of the saints in heaven,

*O blest communion, fellowship divine,*
*We feebly struggle, they in glory shine;*
*Yet all are one in thee, for all are thine.*
*Alleluia!*

I hope that Canon Saville's poems will remind you that we live even today in the world of the saints, and that you will be inspired to let God's light shine through you.

J. JON BRUNO
BISHOP, EPISCOPAL DIOCESE OF LOS ANGELES

# ACKNOWLEDGMENTS

So many dear people have helped create this book about the Saints and Holy Days in the Episcopal church calendar.

My dear wife, Nellie Anne Saville, accompanied me on all the trips to the saints' shrines and encouraged me in innumerable ways.

Thanks to my son, the Rev. John K. Saville III who helped oversee preparations for printing the book, Bob Williams, Janet Kawamoto, and Laura Fisher Smith who oversaw the editing and publishing of the book for the Cathedral Center Press, and the Rt. Rev. Jon Bruno, Bishop of Los Angeles, for writing the foreword and with much gratitude for his support and interest that made the publishing of this book possible. Thanks also to my daughters Susan Remsberg, Debbie Richards, Mary Irvin Baker (lead typist) and daughter-in-law Kathleen Saville for all their help, and especially for being such good "scribes" for the sonnets I dictated while in the hospital. Thanks to son-in-law Bruce Remsberg for selecting many of the hymns and to Darlene Duffield who assisted with some of the typing.

Consultants were Bishop Jon Bruno, Bishop Fred Borsch, retired bishop of Los Angeles, Bishop Robert Anderson, assistant bishop of Los Angeles, Dr. Douglas Eadie, retired professor of religion at the University of Redlands, and Chaplain Lloyd Howard of Plymouth Village in Redlands.

Those finding and taking pictures included Mrs. John Ypma and Dr. Nancy Ypma on five trips across the British Isles and to Moscow and Kiev; Canon Greg Richards and his son, Matthew at Cambridge University; Dr. Erftemeijaer in Swolle, Holland; Mrs.

*Acknowledgments, continued*

Mary Nesamony in Madras, India; Mr. René Arnoud in Lyon, France; Mr. Gastone Squarcia in Milan, Italy; Mrs. Jane Zollner in Memphis Tennesee; The Rev. Marianne Goodman in New Zealand; Mrs Barbara Shuttleworth in Winchester, England; Mrs. Susan Beedie at Canterbury Cathedral, England; Margaret Ypma in Fulda, Germany; Crystal Brittania in Jerusalem; Mr. William Ewald, Greenwich, Connecticut; Wyva Hasselleblad, Senegal and Uganda. Many others provided saints' shrines' pictures. Some did not get into the book, but are in a special family album and in our hearts.

Tours of saints' shrines that I was on were led by Mrs. Cecilia Fryer at St. Paul's, Jarrow, England about St. Bede and Mr. Terry Waite at Lambeth Palace, London, about Thomas Cramner and the first Prayer Book of 1549.

JKS

# CHRISTIAN SAINTS: WE STAND ON THEIR SHOULDERS

At St. Francis of Assisi village, I found the purpose of *Saints in Sonnets*. I had wanted to push on to St. John at Patmos, St. Sophias' cathedral in Istanbul, St. Paul at Philippi, the eastern Mediterranean Christian sanctuaries. My dear wife, Nellie Anne, said we didn't have enough time to absorb it. It would be all rush, rush. She said, "If you must, go ahead, buy the tickets." I hurried on while she came slowly, enjoying the sight of historic Assisi. Next to the ticket office was a little park. I sat down in a chair. Nellie was right. It would be all rush, rush. When she came along I said, "We are not going to do it. You are right."

With time now, we visited the Church of St. Damian's, where Francis imagined the crucifix with Christ's call to build His church. The choir was practicing...angels singing. It was so peaceful and full of faith. Leaving here, we met a Franciscan lay brother. I was moved to tell him of my decision about taking time to enjoy Assisi and not rush from one place to another, but to find God in peace and quiet. Later, I shared our decision with Father Wilbur Washam at "St. Paul's Within the Walls" at Rome. "Assisi does that to you," he said.

All at once my purpose became clear. Sharing the saints and whatever of their holy places of God leads us to, has a power for healing and peace all its own. Now we had time on the rest of the trip to find St. Paul in Rome, St. Augustine's relics, moved to Pavia, St. Irenaeus and the martyrs of Lyons, Thomas Cranmer at Lambeth Palace in London. I remembered moving spiritual experiences when searching for St. Boniface, Archbishop of Mainz, St. Thomas á Kempis in Zwolle, Holland, St. Columba on Iona,

Scotland, St. Patrick at Downpatrick Cathedral in Northern Ireland, and St. Margaret of Scotland's chapel in Edinburgh as spiritual calls to share the love and healing that these heroes and heroines of the faith are still trying to pass on to us.

So these sonnets of the saints hopefully are windows of hope for today from those who have walked with Christ in their particular challenges and faithful efforts for their time. Assisi and these other holy places and persons did that to some degree for me and I trust may do the same for you.

Thanks to all who helped Nellie and me, as listed in the Acknowledgments. Your wisdom, hard work and advice made this book possible.

*Ye blessed souls at rest, who ran this earthly race*
*and now, from sin released, behold the Savior's face,*
*God's praises sound,*
*as in his sight with sweet delight ye do abound.*

*Ye saints, who toil below, adore your heavenly King,*
*and onward as ye go some joyful anthem sing;*
*take what he gives*
*and praise him still through good or ill whoever lives!*
*[Richard Baxter 1615-1691 Hynm 625]*


J. KIMBALL SAVILLE
REDLANDS, CALIFORNIA
NOVEMBER 2003

# THE SONNETS

# GOD THE FATHER

Somewhere beyond the sunrise, Heart of Love
Must share pure joy with love that can respond.
Creation climaxed when first human brow,
Sky-lifted, honored Giver of that bond.
"I am your fathers' God," touched Moses' soul.
His "Let my people go"; they weep and moan
Became glad song of freedom by the sea.
On "Eagles' wings" the Father brings us home.
His prophets shared the promise Heaven sings.
"Thus says the Lord" subdued, inspired kings;
"The Still Small Voice" renewed Elijah's call;
Then Micah's "Justice, mercy, walk with God."
'Til Angel Choirs filled a star-blessed sky;
And cattle stirred with Holy Infant's cry.

# JESUS CHRIST

Your name rings down the ages to my soul.
I see you in the stars of Bethlehem.
I hear you in the winds off Galilee.
I touch you in the hands of every friend.
Why did you pray for me on Olivet?
Why were you scourged for me that Friday noon?
Why plead my ignorance on Calvary,
'Til death was sealed with tears in borrowed tomb?
When Father, Spirit, Son flung out the stars,
And molded Earth for justice mercy, love,
Was not your plan to share high Heaven's joy
With those who trust in you, here and Above?
Oh, Jesus, walk with me each new long day.
Let my brave smiles, for others, point the way.

# THE HOLY SPIRIT

God's Spirit moved across the wat'ry gloom
'Til by Divine Command glad brightness shone.
His Spirit called the soul of Abraham
To seek a Promised Land, a better home.
The Spirit moved, made noble countless lives:
Proud Amos fought for justice from Above;
Isaiah saw the Holiness of God;
Hosea lived forgiveness, Heaven's love;
To Jeremiah, Spirit comes within,
His life his gift, like Man of Galilee.
The Spirit filled the Church at Pentecost
With joy for hearts from guilt and evil free.
Cornelius found his Lord in Peter's word.
The Spirit's healing came when Paul was heard.

# ALL SAINTS

The Lord is glorious in his saints through centuries.
St. Mary Magdalene first saw the risen Lord.
St. Antony helped save the Trinity.
St. Alban saved a British soldier's faith.
St. Patrick saved the Irish people's trust.
Columba brought the gospel Scottish shores.
David saved the faith in ancient Wales.
King Alfred Great saved Britain's faith.
St. Louis IX made dear French faith to flower.
St. Andrew took the faith to Russia's shore.
St. Augustine confessed at mother's knee.
St. Francis brought God's love, what life should be.
The suffragettes helped end dread slavery.
And Martin Luther King died all to free.

*Hymn 287: "For All The Saints Who from Their Labor's Rest"*

# ALL FAITHFUL DEPARTED

A "Cloud of Witnesses" still guide us here
We pray for them, "communion of the saints";
Their love and prayer comes back to us to lift
Our hearts at times when courage weakens, faints
Like Christ's apostles some were canonized
Tall beacon lights, they shine down all the years
Yet others may be dear to us alone;
Our family sweet memories bring tears
All faithful souls departed in the Lord
New Testament calls "saints" and offers prayers;
One does not earn such blessing; faith alone
Will bring us "House of many mansions" there
We walk with dearest loved ones as of old
The Savior's arms still all of us enfold.

*Hymn 358: "Christ the Victorious"*

*November 3*
*Priest, Master theologian of the English Reformation and*
*the Religious Settlement of Queen Elizabeth I in 1559.*
*Author of* The Laws of Ecclesiastical Polity. *Died 1600*

# RICHARD HOOKER

The Puritans and Roman Catholics

Struggled to be the channels of God's grace.

Each meant to share best insights of their faith,

But Queen sought unity with Prayer Book base.

Hooker taught God placed His natural law

In all Creation, making man His own.

So scripture, reason, and tradition, joined

With blest experiences lead us Home.

Our public worship is the surest way

To share our faith, receive support of friends.

Both now and back through centuries of hope

Church family, Christ's Body, never ends.

God's angels will be there to take our prayers

To Him then back again down golden stairs.

*Hymn 522: "Glorious Things of Thee Are Spoken"*

# WILLIBRORD

The Netherlands began to know their Lord,

Cross raised wild northern continent,

When twelve from Britain came with Willibrord,

Brought love of God in Christ, true angels sent.

He won respect of Kings moved by his life.

Of gracious thoughtful care, so full of joy.

Fear ridden pagans, torn by years of strife

Were calmed by faith worst threats could not destroy.

Reaction burned his churches, killed brave priests;

He won some land again and eastward more.

In Denmark thirty slave boys bought and saved;

Fought idols, risked death; opened Christian door.

God blessed this land beside the Zuider Zee,

Our Pilgrim's refuge door, -fore western sea.

*Hymn 534: "God Is Working His Purpose Out"*

# LEO THE GREAT

He faced their savagery, wild Huns;
Persuaded them for tribute now go home.
When Vandals threatened pillage and destroy
Bold stand saved fire, killing, end of Rome
His letter to the Council Chalcedon
The human and divine in Christ are one;
Moved bishops cried, "In Leo, Peter speaks"
Made orthodox this faith for everyone.
Won Church and State endorsement for his claim
As Primate of Church Catholic in West;
In Ages Dark Society he saved
Law, order, culture, much of mankind's best
Leo's most famous Christian work, his *Tome*
Still searching hearts are led to spirit home

*Hymn 565: "He Who Would Valiant Be 'gainst All Disaster"*

# MARTIN

When Rome's proud officer he felt God's call.

At Amiens saw beggar, naked, cold.

In pity ripped his cloak to save a life;

Then his became a Christ-filled story told.

He left the army, came to Poitiers;

Helped Hilary found faith community.

Tours' Bishop, fought for justice, fed the poor;

Built churches, pastored, changed society.

When Christians, heretics and pagans fought

He strove for peace, preached God's all-loving Hand.

Devoted labors carried Christ afar:

Young Patrick trained, new hope for Ireland;

Great Canterbury, Martin's church before;

His cross, Columba's blest Iona shore.

*Hymn 567: "Thine Arm, O Lord, in Days of Old Was Strong to
Heal and Save".*

*November 12*
*Priest, Chaplain to Cambridge and spiritually to*
*the Church of England. Died 1836*

# CHARLES SIMEON

Conversion came when undergraduate;

Required of all, Communion, touched his soul.

He had been told one had to earn this gift;

Thanked God when learned that faith, not law, makes whole;

That character is nurtured by strong faith –

That love of God in Christ wipes out our sin.

Our lives become a love song for the world;

No fears, freed now! We do our best for Him.

He led evangelists who felt God's Call,

Brave missionary Church Society,

Which tried world wide to reach long searching hearts,

Young Martyn died for Persia, India.

"To study Word of God" and share it pure

"Is proper labour of a minister."

*Hymn 422: "Not Far Beyond the Sea"*

# SAMUEL SEABURY

Our Christ sent forth Apostles to the World
To share His saving Gospel's healing love;
They consecrated their successors, called
And blessed by Holy Spirit from above.
Though British chaplain in our Freedom War,
He felt America was now his home.
Soon clergy of Connecticut chose him
To seek a Bishop's orders for their own.
Avoiding oath to serve the English crown,
On north to Aberdeen his prayers now lead.
Free Scottish Bishops gave him ancient role
To pastor all, ordain, God's people feed.
Brought Scottish Prayer of Consecration here;
Communion Spirit blessed, Christ ever near.

*Hymn 359: "God of the Prophets"*

# MARGARET

"Storm-driven north to Scotland's refuge shore,
Sweet prayerful Margaret found for life God's call;
Prince Malcolm, friend before in Edward's court,
Now sought her hand that would his life enthrall.
Six sons, two daughters blessed proud motherhood;
Uncouth but loving husband led towards peace.
Their charities relieved the ill and poor.
She rescued slaves. She sought slave raids to cease.
Her loving cup helped dignify the court,
Trade and learning came from foreign shore.
A deeper worship helped renew the Church.
Columba's isle, Iona, lived once more.
In pain, and grief for Malcolm death, she passed
To Him who promised both home at their last."

*Hymn 304: "I Come With Joy to Meet My Lord"*

# H∪GH

A modest monk, Carthusian, from France,

King Henry called as prior for Somerset;

He turned that struggling Charter House around;

Wise monks and canons joined him, "Heaven sent."

When Lincoln's bishop, saved the city's schools;

Rebuilt cathedral's earthquake damaged life.

Was honored by three Popes – Judge Delegate;

At King's request his justice calmed court strife.

Yet courtiers he gave no rich church posts;

Forbade church funds King Richard's wars, Crusades;

Friend of oppressed, gave lepers tender care;

Risked life to save Jews' lives from mobs wild raids.

King said, "If bishops all were like my lord,

No prince could lift his head against their words."

*Hymn 598: "Lord Christ, When First Thou Cam'st to Earth"*

# HILDA

Felt called to walk God's court of souls in need.

Paulinus, monk of Canterbury, taught,

Baptized her in the Christian faith she sought.

With love she served her uncle's Christian reign

'Til death for Christ brought pagan rule again.

Monastic call, Saint Aidan sensed her gifts:

Devotion, spirit, healing human rifts.

She founded Whitby, Bede said, "Mothered all."

Encouraged poet Caedmon; songs enthrall.

Proud leaders sought her wisdom, counsel, peace;

Her prayerful listening, caring, brought release.

Great Whitby Synod — she backed Celtic Way;

Yet love for Church; agreed Rome's Rule that day.

*Hymn 518: "Christ Is Made the Sure Foundation"*

# ELIZABETH

God's gentle princess was a noble queen;

Three children blessed her Louis and the world.

The helpless, sick and orphans felt her love,

Christ's healing now; prepared for life Above.

With pride she sent her husband knight to war,

But lost him in the Holy Land Crusade.

Heart crushed; then driven from her castle home,

Babe at her breast, she fled in grief alone.

Providing for her children, donned rough robes,

Severe confessor, beatings; still she shared.

Jewels, clothes, gave all for poor, Christ's love revives!

She sewed, nursed, even fished, to save dear lives.

Exhaustion, death, with Louis evermore;

What cross of glory borne 'til twenty-four!

*Hymn 605: "What Does the Lord Require? Do Justly*
*Love Mercy Walk Humbly with Your God"*

# EDMUND

He rests at great monastery, "Bury St. Edmunds"
"He served his people, humble and devout;
Was always mindful of the counsel, 'If a chief
Yourself exalt not, live as one of them.'
He cared for poor and widows, all in grief."
Invading Danes demanded he submit
To Danish law and custom, share his rule.
Firm answer, "'Til Hingwar shall bow to Christ
I'll never bow to him, so pagan cruel."
They seized Edmund and bound him to a tree;
They tortured him with darts. They would not cease;
Between the blows he called on Jesus Christ;
They could not break his faith 'til death brought peace.[1]
He died for Christian hope in world so rough.
Dane's hearts were touched for God. Love said "Enough."

[1] *Aelfric, Abbot of Eynsham in* They Still Speak
*By J. Robert Wright, 1993.*

*Hymn 552: "Fight the Good Fight With All Thy Might"*

# CLEMENT

Companion of Saint Peter and Saint Paul,

Freed slave who witnessed their brave martyrdom,

Third bishop of most persecuted Church,

Which was Rome's hope and strength, hard years to come.

He pastored tenderly that martyred flock;

With Peter's boldness souls for Christ would find;

With Paul's Damascus vision taught the faith;

And preached, as both, Christ's care for all mankind.

Like Scriptures wrote to Paul's Corinthians:

"Be subject to your neighbor; share his needs;

Strong care for weak and weak respect the strong;

The wise show wisdom, not in words but deeds."

"The grace of Jesus Christ be with you all.

In faith receive and live God's loving call."

*Hymn 24: "The Day Thou Gavest, Lord, Is Ended"*

# JAMES OTIS SARGENT HUNTINGTON

Served Church for working class in Syracuse.

Retreat in Philadelphia deep "Call";

"Religious" life of Eucharist, work, prayer.

At mission, Holy Cross, love care helped all.

New York's East Side poor immigrants felt Christ.

There pastored youth's sad plight and desperate needs;

Gave life to social witness of the Church.

The Labor Movement, single tax found seeds.

Now, Order Holy Cross vocations gained;

Their monastery mother house, West Park.

Superior, led call to faithfulness;

For Anglican "Religious" Life strong mark.

While preaching, teaching lifted thoughts Above;

Wrote, "Holiness is brightness of God's love."

*Hymn 660: "O Master Let Me Walk With Thee in*
*Lovely Paths of Service Free"*

# KAMEHAMEHA & EMMA

They sought a faith that honored heritage,

Aloha's ancient meaning, "God in you."

The king translated Prayer Book for his land.

As childhood friends they married Anglican;

Chose son's godmother, Queen Victoria;

Then his young death; the king's soon sad demise!

Crushed Emma helped first Bishop Stanley's call,

The great Cathedral, her Queens Hospital,

Christ centered schools, her people's lives to mend;

Queen Lilioukalani, dear friend,

Betrayed, imprisoned, our church cared, sustained.

Archbishop, Emma's "saintly soul" acclaimed.

Their vacant throne, Aloha's memory;

Their noble spirit still moves you and me.

*Hymn 537: "Christ for the World We Sing!"*

# ST. ANDREW

Blue Galilee saw glory one great day
When Jesus called bold brothers to His side.
Soon Andrew's soul was moved by Jordan's bank
As "See the Lamb of God!" the Baptist cried.
He followed, found his Lord, brought Peter too.
The wide world's faith has never been the same.
Child's lunch he brought to Christ, fed multitude;
Yet pain would come for owning that dear name.
When Easter night he saw his Risen Lord,
Christ's "Go to all the world" fulfilled deep goals.
He sought more brothers, north, wild Scythia;
When bound to cross still preached, won caring souls.
St. Andrew's, Scotland, Angel placed his shrine;
Their patron saint inspires your faith and mine.

*Hymn 549: "Jesus Calls Us O'r the Tumult"*

# NICHOLAS FERRAR

He sought to make Christ's gift of peace more known;

With family, friends withdrew to pray and care.

Restored neglected church near manor home;

Rejoiced rich Prayer Book life and worship there;

Taught school and gave the children extra love;

Helped heal and feed the poor their neighborhood.

Their books of faith were lanterns from Above;

Wrote moral stories; lifted all they could.

When still a youth faced death, poured out his soul;

"Most dearest parents if God take me now,"

Grieve not for with Christ I shall see life whole."

To Him who is above all worlds we bow.

Such character blessed their community.

Revived Faith Orders knew this ministry.

*Hymn 410: "Praise My Soul The King of Heaven, To His Feet*
*Thy Tribute Bring"*

# CHANNING MOORE WILLIAMS

He felt God's call to reach the Orient.

Two years in China, then he sought Japan.

Called "foreign devil," still he was content

To live and study humbly as Christ's man.

His patient caring won their confidence.

Now free to start a school Divinity;

Faith power drew souls, spirit's, sense;

Was future St. Paul's University.

Made Bishop of Japan and China too

St. Luke's new Hospital brought healing care.

When joined with British mission life renewed –

Called Nippon Sei Ko Kai, long years his prayer.[1]

His Japanese friends wrote on his gravestone,

"Taught fifty years Christ's ways and not his own."

[1] *The Holy Catholic Church of Japan*

*Hymn 636: "How Firm a Foundation Ye Saints of the Lord"*

*December 4*
*Priest and Monk, Champion of Orthodox Christianity,*
*Doctor of the Universal Church. Died* c. *760*

# JOHN OF DAMASCUS

Renouncing wealth and comfort safe court post,

Found peace, monk's life, calm wilderness Dead Sea.

Sought Christ in Scriptures, early fathers' prayer;

Helped save historic faith for you and me;

Real Presence of Divine in Eucharist.

The veneration Mother of our Lord,

For sacred pictures, icons, deep respect;

They represent Our God, alone adored.

What trust for life eternal his great hymns!—

"The Day of resurrection tell abroad";

"Thou hallowed chosen morn of praise, that best";

And "Come ye faithful raise the strain," for God!

"The victory over death revealed," he taught.

His Fount of Knowledge, tells God's World he sought.

*Hymn 363: "Ancient of Days"*

*December 5*
*Priest, Early Scholar and Apologist*
*Died* C. *210*

# CLEMENT OF ALEXANDRIA

"Lord ministers all good and all our help

Both as man and as God—forgiving sins;

And as man, training us away from sins.

So man is therefore justly dear to God." [1]

He saw philosophers prepare Christ's way.

"Plato alludes to god, around the king—

Are all things; He is—cause of all good things" [2]

Bold prophets, "Do I not fill Heaven and Earth?" [3]

If music is the language of the soul,

His songs lift hearts our Savior Christ to laud—

"Sunset to sunrise changes now for God—

Makes world anew—Redeemer's thorn-crowned brow." [4]

Our God said, "Out of Egypt have I called my son" [5]

Here Jesus' refuge, Clement's faith, Mark's martyrdom.

[1] The Instructor, *Chapter 3*
[2] Exhortation to the Heathen, *chapter 6*
[3] *Ibid., Chapter 8; Jeremiah 23:23*
[4] Hymnal 1982, *no. 163*
[5] *Hosea 11:1, Matthew 2:15*

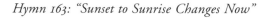

*Hymn 163: "Sunset to Sunrise Changes Now"*

# NICHOLAS

Devoted parents brought him to the Lord.

When orphaned, Bishop, Uncle, took him home.

Ordained, made pilgrimage to Holy Land;

Where Jesus walked found peace, dear Christ his own.

Dream angel called him to return and share.

Monastic life appealed, but call again;

In Myra sought seclusion; prayed god's Will.

Made Bishop there to shepherd souls of men.

Nine years imprisoned, tortured for his Lord,

'Til freed by Constantine, faith's victory.

Nicaea's Council, fought for Christ Divine;

When jailed again the Savior set him free.

Lost sailors, children loved his saving care.

His soul in Christmas makes our world more fair.

*Hymn 99: "Go Tell It on the Mountain —*
*That Jesus Christ Is Born"*

# AMBROSE

"Make Ambrose Bishop!" desperate people cried.

The riot quelled by Governor's demand,

Both Catholics' and Arians' respect

Moved noble heart. This Call was God's Command!

Divesting privilege and worldly wealth,

Kept open house, received each troubled soul.

Preached fearlessly the Apostolic Faith;

Sweet words of Grace made proud Augustine whole.

Defied the Empress' seizure of his church;

The Emperor who killed made penitent.

Gervase, Protase, first martyrs' shrine revered;

Within Ambrogia, his monument.

His grand "Te Deum," hymns our spirits' thrill.

Courageous loving footsteps echo still.

*Hymn 233: "The Eternal Gifts of Christ the King"*

# LUCY

An innocent young maiden found her Lord;
Gave marriage dowry to the sick and poor.
Her jilted fiancé exposed her faith.
Seized by the State, refused each frightful lure.
A brothel's horror lastly was her fate:
She fought to save her honor, died by sword.
Yet Christians everywhere felt brave new hope,
That souls are safe with God in Christ adored.
Her relics came to rest by Venice shore
Where gondoliers still sing of peace and love,
Bless "Sancta our Lucia evermore."
Her name fills hearts with peace from Heaven above.
A lamp her symbol, she the patroness
Of health for eyes, our sight to heal and bless.

*Hymn 699: "Jesus, Love of My Soul, Let Me in Thy Bosom Fly"*

*December 21, Early Tradition – Preached in Malabar, India.*
*Martyred and buried at Mylapore, Ancient stone cross,*
*where his body rested before being transported to Edessa 394.*
*Another tradition says he is still buried at San Tome, India.*

# ST. THOMAS, THE APOSTLE

He kept on loyally through every doubt.
When Jesus went to Lazarus, he cried,
"Then let us go that we may die with Him."
When Jesus promised life to those who died,
"You know the Way," torn puzzled Thomas said,
"We know not where you go, how know the way?"
Glad Easter night, but Thomas wasn't there;
Still troubled heart for him on Easter Day.
When week had passed was with the Ten once more.
The Lord appeared, "See! Touch my hands and side."
Thomas knelt on trembling knees, "My Lord! My God!"
Flashed round the earth — God loves all, saving tide.
"Because you have seen, Thomas, you believe;
Blest those who have not seen and yet believe."

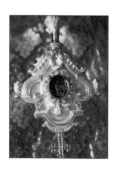

*Hymn 58: "Lo! He Comes With Clouds Descending"*

# ST. STEPHEN

His face shone like an angel as he preached
God's leading of His peoples' destiny;
But hardened by sly charges, pressured, false,
Sanhedrin sought for hint of blasphemy.
As deacon he had served the sick and poor
With food from offerings and healing care.
His witness won new converts for His Lord;
So envy also caused cruel seizure there.
He said, "You killed The Righteous One"; they fumed.
Then Stephen looked to Heaven, joyous, cried,
"Look! See God and Jesus standing by."
They rushed him; seized him; stoned him 'til he died.
Last words "Lord, lay not this sin to their charge."
Such faith shocked angry souls, It's spread how large!

*Hymn 73: "The King Shall Come When Morning Dawns"*

# ST. JOHN

He lay on Jesus' breast that Thursday Eve,

When bread and wine were blessed eternal food.

He took dear Mary home to be her son

With Jesus died upon the Holy Rood.

Forbidden, flogged, yet still he taught the Word;

When Peter in the Temple healed the lame.

They laid their hands and brought the Spirit gift

When Philip baptized in the Saviour's name.

John's Gospel glows with dear Christ's saving power;

Epistles call men's hearts to caring love.

His Revelation lifts our Christian hope

Of crosses changed in brave new life above.

From Ephesus still hear his saving call,

"Love one another, children, God loves all."

*Hymn 335: "I Am the Bread of Life"*

# THE HOLY INNOCENTS

Augustine called them "buds killed by the frost
Of persecution, moment showed themselves."
The Wisemen told King Herod New King of Jews
He feared mysterious rival Bible tells.
"To find this infant king; then let me know;
So I can worship him, "he slyly said."
But Wisemen saw thru evil jealousy
From Bethlehem another way home led.
Cruel Herod killed all infants Bethlehem,
But Joseph, angel warned, took Mary, child
To Egypt's shelter 'til the throne had changed;
Then Nazareth for boyhood safe and mild.
May World-wide church protect young innocence;
God's children help bring caring, peace, more sense.

*Hymn 246: "In Bethlehem a New Born Boy Was Hailed"*

# THOMAS BECKET

A gifted youth was blessed by God and Man
Theology, a Deacon, Canon Law.
When Henry II made him chancellor
Helped King's ambitions every way he saw.
When Archbishop of Canterbury – changed!
No more would church help pay for foreign wars;
No more would civil laws rule clergy lives;
Appealed to Pope to open freedom doors.
Returned from French exile with fragile truce;
Yet still refused, fought king's supremacy.
"Who will rid me of this priest?" Henry cried.
Four barons slew him, last words, "Willingly
I die for Jesus in the church defense."
Cathedral round walked king in penitence.

*Hymn 559: "Lead Us, Heavenly Father, Lead Us"*

# HOLY NAME

Eight days from birth, received his special Name,
Jesus true man God's sacrifice for sins.
Remembering God's words the angels said,
"For he shall save his people from their sins."
Because Lord raised from cross on Easter day
Our sins assuaged earth's torment goes away
We reigned with him in Glory just the same;
Our blessed hope the power of the Name.
We are the builders, new world saving grace.
For everyone there is his own dear place.
Then dawn shall come, a servant-world of hope;
Faith power by day, by night the faith to cope.
Thank you dear Lord for Jesus, gift to all;
For power to build your kingdom for us all.

*Hymn 252: "Jesus! Name of Wondrous Love!"*

# JULIA CHESTER EMERY

Entire family shared the love of Christ.

Two brothers, priests and pastors, gave their best.

Sweet Helen cared for sister invalid,

And kept a home for missionary's rest.

Strong Mary led auxiliary's dream

Of mission service home and foreign field.

Of this dear Julia was the instrument;

Exhausting labors, wondrous harvest yield;

Church deaconess helped make canonical

United Thank Offering of action prayers

With healing care made Gospel message full.

"Miss Julia," to a grateful church you gave

So many ways for Jesus' love to save!

*Hymn 537: "Christ for the World We Sing!"*

# WILLIAM LAUD

Devoted, dedicated priest of God;

He sought for values out of step with times;

Lost medieval rituals brought back.

The right of kings to rule, God's gift Divine.

He emphasized the priesthood, sacraments.

To reverence the altar asked up all;

Returned it to the east wall as of old;

Bring people humble to church life, his call.

Defended common peasants 'gainst land lords.

Sought independent church from Parliament.

Extremists called it treason; soon impeached.

Five years of pain, beheaded; land was rent.

He made a noble end: "The Lord receive

My soul, and bless this kingdom, charity and peace." [1]

[1] Lesser Feasts and Fasts

*Hymn 236: "King of the Martyrs' Noble Band"*

# AELRED

Cistercian abbot, author, led with care
His Order's loving healing for the soul.
His gentle holiness, discretion wise
Attracted men, his character their goal.
Rievaulx grew largest monastery home;
Foundations new rough England, Scotland blest.
Concern for poor and troubled spread with love;
Saints John, Augustine his brave life confessed.
Westminster wept at his eloquence
When Edward the Confessor's tomb moved there.
Last years in pain still pastored far-flung flock;
His reconciling gifts the ages share.
Wrote Edward's life, Isaiah's faith and hope;
How friendship lifts the heart with strength to cope.

*Hymn 714: "Shalom, My Friends"*

# HILARY

Proud brilliant pagan lawyer loved the truth;

The Scriptures satisfied his questing soul;

His yearning spirit found God's peace divine;

As bishop fought to save Christ's Savior role.

The Arians denied Nicaea's Creed;

Their Lord was not the Word before all days.

At councils he stood like a "cedar firm";

Jerome and Augustine gave him such praise.

When banished for his faith to Phrygia,

From lonely exile still inspired his flock.

Two years he taught with love on journey home;

Then wife and daughter died, worst painful shock.

Once more, Milan's great Council, gave his best;

Time called him Athanasius of the West.

*Hymn 362: "Holy, Holy, Holy"*

# ANTHONY

"Go sell all that thou hast, come follow me."
This Gospel called a gentle youth to God.
He found in desert solitude Christ's peace;
The love that filled his life would never cease.
For years the sad and troubled sought his help.
His counsel wise and sweet calmed each torn heart;
They settled 'round his cell to learn God's love.
In simple living joy came from Above.
In Alexandria he helped the brave.
Shared faith with martyrs facing last grim trials;
Upheld the Creed, refuted Arians;
Affirmed the Son and Father ever One.
Was led to Paul of Thebes, laid him to rest;
In Anthony's soul-steps are many blest.

*Hymn 423: "Immortal, Invisible, God Only Wise"*

# CONFESSION OF ST. PETER

Apostle's trust and love through all his years;
Rough fisherman, Christ called to fish for men.
So moved by Master's care for human tears,
Inspires faith and hope, both now as then.
Began with, "Thou, Messiah, Son of God";
Saw Jesus blessed 'neath Holy Mountain skies.
Gethsemane – sweat drops on sacred sod;
Denied Him; wept before those loving eyes.
He fled the trial, hid from the shameful Cross;
Yet breathless ran to Easter garden tomb.
Ecstatic joy that night transformed the loss;
"Go feed my sheep!" New spirit life would bloom.
He healed the sick, raised dead in Jesus' name;
He preached to Rome; the world was never same.

*Hymn 254: "You Are the Christ, O Lord"*

# WULFSTAN

A humble priest declined his bishopric;
Chose monastery, serving poor and sick.
Invasion threat; again came bishop call;
Accepted, stood a rock at England's fall.
King Harold and his bowmen died in vain.
Proud William Conqueror began harsh reign,
The Anglo-Saxons cruelly to oppress
'Til Wulfstan fought to ease their worst distress.
Though risking life he dared to face the King,
Archbishop Lanfranc too, for help to bring:
Relief for serfs, church laymen's rights to save,
No English youth again an Irish slave.
'Til death, brought hope, himself near poverty,
With Gospel, Sacraments, love ministry.

*Hymn 594: "God of Grace and God of Glory"*

*January 20*
*Martyr at Rome, died* C. *300*
*(on the cover)*

# SEBASTIAN

A handsome Gaul that served the emperor

A member of his guard Pretorian

Authorities found out forbidden faith

Illegally he was a Christian

His torture sentence tiny arrows shot

With faith and courage faced his awful end

The arrows failed for mercy never pled

They bludgeoned him to death his faith to rend

They buried him beside the Appian Way;

Same place Apostle Paul gave up his life

How many heroes, heroines since then

Have laid down lives for right in holy strife?

Lord, come with Grace; turn human hearts to peace.

May Love and Spirit angered hearts release.

*Hymn 236: "King of the Martyrs' Noble Band"*

# FABIAN

New Bishop to be chosen, solemn day;

The great assembly knelt in hope to pray;

So many leaders strong, which one, O Lord?

Just then white dove beneath the ceiling soared;

It fluttered down and lighted on one head,

No priest, wise layman, Fabian, instead.

Like Christ's Baptism, Holy Spirit Dove,

All cried, "He's worthy!" Sign from God above.

He led with faith in church of Peter, Paul;

Dispatched brave missionaries, first to Gaul;

Wrote Origin and Cyprian, his guides;

Named deacon to record the martyrs' lives.

In Decius persecution gave his life.

Christ stands beside His own in noble strife.

*Hymn 241: "Hearken to the Anthem Glorious of the*
*Martyr Robed in White"*

# AGNES

Proud Diocletian feared the Christian tide;

Forced all once more to deify the throne;

Yet one brave girl held firm her childhood faith;

The only one true God would be her own.

Her beauty, gentle innocence drew men.

Betrothed to Christ forever, her reply.

The prefect's son, rejected for her hand,

In anger sought her will to break or die.

Though placed in brothel no one dared approach;

Her spirit shield of light no man could break.

Then cry of witch condemned her to the flames,

But sword alone her pure, sweet life could take.

Each year two lambs are shorn of soft white wool:

Archbishops' palliums from Agnes' soul.

*Hymn 343: "Shepherd of Souls, Refresh and Bless"*

# VINCENT

The Christian persecutions neared their end
When Diocletion ordered torture, grave
For those who would not worship Roman gods,
A fearful challenge to the faithful brave.
Jailed with his bishop in Valencia,
Then ordered to renounce their faith or die,
Valerius, with speech impediment
Told Vincent, "Preach our Christ we can't deny!"
When Dacian, the Governor, heard plea,
With face like Stephen's at his stoning fate,
His fury grew, exiled Valerius;
Told Vincent, "Leave your Christ or violent fate."
Racked, torn, burnt slowly on a griddle fire,
His witness moves our souls; our hearts inspire.

*Hymn 236: "King of the Martyrs' Noble Band"*

# PHILLIPS BROOKS

"Two aspects of the work of ministry" –
The "message" preached or written, of the Son;
Our "witness" lived, as we feel Christ within;
So "truth and personality" merge one. [1]
He preached as friend might speak to a dear friend.
Three truths he taught – God lives in you and me;
Man, child of God for Blessedness;
Christ shows what God is and what man may be. [2]
His church in Boston burned, a total loss.
Four years his members grew in places bare.
Business leaders came to hear him, noon;
The whole community felt love and care.
World loves "O Little Town of Bethlehem" [3] —
It's faith and caring, soul of this great man.

[1] *Lectures of Preaching 1877, quoted in*
They Still Speak, *J. R. Wright*
[2] Westminister Dictionary of Church
History, *p. 133*
[3] Hymnal 1982, *pp. 78-79*

*Hymn 79: "O Little Town of Bethlehem"*

# CONVERSION OF ST. PAUL

The Great Commission was renewed, set free
When chastened Saul, rememb'ring Stephen's stand,
Cried out in humbled awe, "Who art Thou, Lord?"
And felt His love in Annanias' hand.
What pain for ransomed Paul at Martyr's grave!
What strength from Barnabas' and Peter's trust!
What courage to uphold God's equal Grace!
What faith divine, as though with Heaven discussed!
He strove to reach the world as Jesus said:
Dear Antioch, Wise Greece, Imperial Rome.
His caring heart made real new life in Christ.
His God-filled mind led countless seekers home.
Paul's vision calls through all man's fever'd years:
God's love in Christ redeems all human tears.

*Hymn 255: "We Sing the Glorious Conquest"*

# TIMOTHY & TITUS

Glad dreams and longings call a man to God;

Call also friends to help along life's way.

As Paul preached Christ and searching hearts were awed

Young Timothy, life changed, found his great day.

For years he followed, sharing joy and pains;

Spoke for his mentor, Greece and Ephesus.

When Bishop there, fought godless pagan, claims;

Faith healings at his shrine, Christ's blessedness.[1]

Paul wrote to Titus, "in faith my true son";[2]

Sent him to Crete; find elders for God's call, –

"Considerate with love for everyone."[3]

"Greet those who love us; Grace be with you all."

His sons in spirit gave their lives for friends

How many hearts their witness new life sends!

[1] *St. Jerome and St. John at Constantinople*
   *in* Oxford Dictionary of Saints 1978,
   *David Farmer*
[2] *Titus 1:4*
[3] *Ibid 1:6*

*Hymn 244: "Come Pure Hearts—Sing of*
   *Those Who Spread the Treasure"*

# JOHN CHRYSOSTOM

When Holy John was called from Antioch,

Constantinople's bishopric to fill,

He preached God's love and charity to all.

Then championed pure virtue, fought grave ill.

With austere life and care of sick and poor,

The common people loved their pastor friend.

Yet Empress and her court, shocked by his truth,

Let bogus council falsehoods bring his end.

Deposed, recalled by common folk, outraged,

Again he preached devout self-giving life.

But royalty could not accept Christ's way,

Condemned their Saint to exile's pain and strife.

The Caucasus became a martyr's tomb.

From virtue's ashes change, new faith would bloom.

*Hymn 335: "I Am the Bread of Life"*

*January 28*
*Priest and Friar, named "Teacher of the Church." Next to Augustine*
*perhaps the greatest Theologian in the history of Western Christianity.*
*Died 1274*

# THOMAS AQUINAS

When Aristotle's science was preserved

By manuscripts monks copied thousand years.

Faith – reason conflict threatened heart of Church;

For Aristotle truth just what appears.

But Thomas sought the truth of trust in God.

Like Moses telling Pharaoh God's commands,

"Now let my people go." But Pharaoh cried,

"What is the name of Him who so demands?"

"What shall I say?" pled Moses; Lord replied,

Tell Pharaoh, "I am who I am" sent you.

So God is Being, brings all life to be!

And nature's "reasons" show Creator too.

Yet Incarnation and the Trinity

By Revelation only can we see.

*Hymn 311: "O Saving Victim"*

# BRIGID

Tradition tells her caring loving life.

When mother, slave, was sold by father's wife

And Druids raised her, she helped feed the poor;

Led troubled, blind, kept sheep safe on the moor.

Baptized by Patrick, shared Christ she adored;

Won Druid family to love the Lord.

Their father, now a Christian, set her free;

Said, "Kine that thou hast milked I offer thee."

"No kine," she said, "my mother's freedom give!"

She founded Abbey, helped distressed to live

With faith and hope all over Ireland;

"Was prayerful, patient, glad in God's command."

Of poets, blacksmiths, healers patroness,

Her churches Europe wide her love confess.

*Hymn 541: "Come Labor On"*

# THE PRESENTATION OF OUR LORD IN THE TEMPLE

When Mary, Joseph brought their first born Son,

Presenting Him to God, the Holy One,

Her life was purified by giving all,

Her dearest treasure for moved hearts to call.

Like Exodus, fulfilling ancient law,

His Presentation fills our souls with awe,

Did not the sons of Israel feel care

When Egypt's slaves were freed, Passover there?

Then Simeon proclaimed the Child "a light

To lighten Gentiles," bring the world Christ sight,

Sweet Anna, Prophetess, foretold for Child

His saving grace, redemption, love, peace mild

A new and perfect offering had come

God's sacrificial Lamb for everyone.

*Hymn 259: "Hail to the Lord Who Comes"*

# ANSKAR

When Vikings ravaged Britain, seeds were sown
That flowered when brave Saxon saint felt "Call"
To reach for Christ fierce Scandinavians;
Voice said, "Though crowned with martyrdom" seek all.
When Harold, King of Denmark sought God's help
First Christian school with courage he began.
When local pagans rough, new vision came,
"Declare the word of God to every man."
Then Emperor of France sent him to tell
Remotest Sweden of God's loving Grace.
King Borgn was moved, let Anscar preach his Christ;
How prayer and love bring close the Master's face.
"Apostle ours" the Northlands call Him still.
For Denmark, "Patron Saint" who lived God's will.

*Hymn 676: "There Is a Balm in Gilead"*

# CORNELIUS

An angel told Cornelius "Send your men
To Peter now at Joppa by the sea."
As Peter prayed an angel told him, "Watch,
Cornelius wants your help for Christ to see."
Said Peter, "Jews and Gentiles do not fraternize;
We do not eat their food; it is not pure."
God said, "No creature heaven made call thou impure;
Three men are knocking, go their faith ensure."
When Peter came Cornelius said, "Now tell
What God has asked for you to say and share."
So Peter preached the Gospel to large crowd;
God's spirit fell on them with loving care.
"Your faith has made you Christians," Peter cried,
"Now all you faithful here shall be baptized."[1]

[1] *Acts 10*

*Hymn 99: "Go Tell It on the Mountain"*

# THE MARTYRS OF JAPAN

In Fifteen Forty Nine Christ first made known

By Francis Xavier, brave Jesuit.

Three Hundred Thousand soon the Savior's own;

'Til fear of foreign pressures brought fierce ban.

The captain of jailed shipwrecked crew defied;

Warned, "Free them or face secret Christian force."

His twenty-six, Franciscans, crucified

While calling to each other, "Trust the Lord!"

Heroic Paul preached love from cross that day,

"I Pardon Emperor, and all, for death;

Salvation only comes the Christian Way;

Seek baptism and live for Christ yourselves."

Soon thousands exiled, tortured, speared or drowned.

Two centuries, no clergy, faith still found!

*Hymn 561: "Stand Up Stand Up for Jesus"*

*February 13*
*Priest, Dedicated Black American pastor*
*Died 1818*

# ABSALOM JONES

"By rivers Babylon we sat and wept

When we remembered Zion" like cries here – [1]

Lost homes in Africa, lost loves, torn hearts

And torn our country 'til freed slaves, no fear.

He taught himself to read New Testament.

When sixteen sold in Philadelphia;

Now family lost, at night school learned to write;

Could send his mother, brothers, sister love.

At twenty married, earned to set wife free;

Himself as well; faith God would save distressed.

Ordained by Bishop White he founded church,

St. Thomas; preached God's care for poor, oppressed.

His greatest gift was healing pastor's care;

Beloved by his own flock, and city there.

[1] *From Psalm 137 prescribed for Absalom Jones*
   *Day, February 13; and Jones' sermon January 1,*
   *1808, in thanksgiving for the abolition of the*
   *African slave trade.*

*Hymn 529: "In Christ There Is No East or West,*
      *In Him No South or North"*

# CYRIL & METHODIUS

St. Paul brought Christ to Greece; His spirit moved

From Thessalonica to reach the Slavs.

Blessed brothers born and priested there were sent

By patriarch to reach Moravians.

Their king sought Slavic teachers of the faith.

They taught God's Word but found no alphabet.

Cyril made first one for Bible, Liturgy;

Began a written culture, down the years.

Opposed by Arians, sought help from Pope;

Brought Clement's relics, martyred saint of Rome.

Pope Adrian so honored all their work —

Ordained them Bishops — lead more souls Christ's own.

Cyril died, Methodius returned, shared love;

All things for all "led hearts" to Heaven above.

*Hymn 544: "Jesus Shall Reign Where-e'er the Sun"*

*February 15*
*Priest and Missionary, Humanitarian and Educator,*
*The Bishop of London's Commissary to Maryland. Died 1730*

# THOMAS BRAY

He championed our Church Colonial.

Great need for educated priests, hearts taught.

Most Christians were too poor for their support [1]

Yet parents, youth and children Spirit sought.

He founded lending libraries and schools.

He raised new funds for missionary aims;

Influenced English priests America.

Concerned for Indians, black slaves, their pains.

Great gift was founding two societies –

"Promoting Christian knowledge" foreign lands

And for the "Propogation of the Gospel" Faith;

Two hundred eighty years their caring stands.

Deplorable home prisons, moved appeal;

Touched Church's conscience, will to save and heal.

[1] They Still Speak *by M. Robert Wright, p. 40*

*Hymn 609: "Where Cross the Crowded Ways of Life"*

# MARTIN LUTHER

Prophetic life that echoes down the years;

Faith grows and lives in "Bible, word of God"

He fought that spirit trap, indulgences;

Pay money to the church for sins is fraud.

Refusing to recant, named heretic.

He called the Church to ethical reform;

The Christian's right to freedom from Church bonds;

Justification by one's faith, reborn.

At Worms the Diet said, "Go burn your books."

His fateful words, "Unless I am Convinced

By Scriptures or by reason I cannot –

God help me!" Brave stand healed souls ever since.

For many fearful hearts he led the way;

Courageous lives of witness every day.

*Hymn 687: "A Mighty Fortress Is Our God"*

# POLYCARP

"I saw John share God's love in Ephesus;

He built on faith foundations Paul had laid.

Sweet Mary's home was comfort to us all;

The Spirit drew us, changed us; Christ had saved.

John consecrated me for Smyrna's flock;

I learned from others who had seen the Lord.

Ignatius' letter on his martyr's path

Renewed my trust to share the Spirit's sword.

Rome's Anicetus heeded our concern;

Preserved Christ's body, love of East with West.

Brave Ireneaus I ordained for Gaul;

Broad grasp of faith with missionary zest.

Soon Stephen's way will call to heavenly joy;

Pray God the flames will not my faith destroy."

*Hymn 558: "Faith of Our Fathers"*

# ST. MATTHIAS

Eleven prayed yet still felt incomplete.
Had not the Lord called twelve to share His Light?
Still sad and hurt by Judas' treachery;
Hard to forget that grim betrayal night.
Then Peter stood, "It's written in the Psalms –
Another take his place of leadership –
Choose one who has been with us the whole time"
Christ's Resurrection faith, Messiahship.
Two named; by lot Matthias joined the rest.
Twelve ready now for "Spirit's Ecstasy"
Tradition says he preached Judea first,
Then Cappadocia near the Caspian Sea.
Helena, Empress, relics took to Rome
Where Paul and Peter sleep, their martyrs' home.

*Hymn 231: "By All Your Saints Still Striving"*

# GEORGE HERBERT

It was a tense and rough rebellious time
Sad strife with Puritans and Anglicans.
King Charles named rector, saintly George,
To cures in Fugglestone and Bremerton.
A model pastor – priest he calmed men's hearts
To lift their souls toward peace, and trust in God
Folks "let their plows rest" when his saints – bell rang
That they might offer prayers with him to God.
Taught nothing is small service for Our Lord;
Reminded Christians ever since that all
We do in daily life both small and great
Are ways to serve and worship, meet His call.
His poetry still makes our hearts to ring,
"Let all the World in every corner sing."

*Hymn 403: "Let All the World in Every Corner Sing"*

# DAVID

When Rome drew back from England, chaos reigned.

Invading pagans' terror brought wild fear.

The threatened church withdrew to refuge Wales;

Then God-called saint revived the faithful here.

As David means "beloved" so he loved

With patient discipline each monk he led.

When Bishop, caring monasteries spread,

Peace isles of hope where brave young souls were fed.

He fought Pelagius' subtle heresy:

No Cross, men save themselves, just hold Christ's hand;

Made pilgrimage to walk where Jesus walked;

Trained Irish saints to help their precious land.

From Galilee to Britain's hallowed shore

Such shoulders we dare stand on evermore.

*Hymn 610: "Lord, Whose Love Through Humble*
*Service Bore the Weight of Human Need"*

# CHAD

St. Aidan trained him Holy Island's shore;

He lived the Celtic way, old Britain's gift.

When Whitby's council chose the Roman way,

Accepted humbly, healing Christian rift;

Resigned York's see for Wilfrid, Rome's new choice;

Said, "Never thought I'm worthy of such place."

This holy man church called to Lichfield then,

Walked his whole diocese, brought Christ's sweet grace.

Archbishop sent him off, long forest trails.

Dear pastor to each far off lonely soul.

Built monastary; taught with vibrant faith,

A Church of truth, prayer, purity his goal.

Heard angel song, came to His Lord in peace;

Urged friends, "Prepare" God's love will never cease.

*Hymn 659: "O Master, Let Me Walk With Thee*
*in Lowly Paths of Service Free"*

# JOHN &
# CHARLES WESLEY

They sought the Lord, in earnest faithful prayer;

They sought Him in the New World's "harvest" field;

Returned, they found Him with Moravians

While Luther's thoughts on Romans, faith revealed.

John said, "I felt my heart was strangely warmed.

I felt I trusted Christ and Christ alone.

He took away my sins, yes even mine;

And saved me from the law of sin and death."

They brought God's love to cruelly burdened lives.

They fought that heartless torture, slavery trade.

They preached in streets and fields to hopeless poor.

Their caring helped class warfare dangers fade.

John's sermons brought the Gospel, made lives whole.

Charles' hymns still lift to God the Christian soul.

*Hymn 535: "Ye Servants of God, Your Master Proclaim"*

# PERPETUA &
# HER COMPANIONS

She could not worship emperor divine.

Though father pled she spoke for Christ, her own,

"I am a Christian, worship only God."

Her nursing son forced to her parents' home.

They prayed for strength in dungeon darkness cold.

Felicitas' newborn torn from her care;

Last kiss, sweet daughter placed in sister's arms.

For death Perpetua helped all prepare.

While mangled by fierce leopard, boar and bear,

Companions saw her tossed by savage cow;

Heard last brave cry, "Stand fast in faith and love!

Our torment must not cause your faith to bow."

Christ took them after one last kiss of peace.

Their prison visions still our faith increase.

*(For their vision dreams see* Ante Nicene Fathers
*Volume 3, pp. 699 – 706)*

*Hymn 238: "Blessed Feasts of Blessed Martyrs"*

# GREGORY OF NYSSA

A long hard road to glory bravely trod,

Third Cappadocian Father, Saint of God.

Famed relics, Forty Martyrs of Sebaste,

Inspired this youth lector for the Church.

Called by his brother, Basil, was ordained;

As Nyssa's bishop, Nicene faith maintained.

Yet Arian's false theft charge drove him out,

Forced two years' hiding 'til their final rout.

Mourned Basil and Macrina, sister dear,

Her faith sustained by his, within his arms.

Found utter truth in Jesus, Savior, Lord;

Wrote movingly of God in Christ adored.

Constantinople's Council thus proclaimed;

Then "Pillar of the Church" him proudly named.

*Hymn 364: "O God We Praise Thee and Confess"*

# GREGORY THE GREAT

Vast gifts for Christians ever since began
When Roman Prefect took his cloistered vows.
Proud Constantinople's court next felt his love;
As Pope gave all that human strength allows.
The Church remained a rock when Rome was lost:
Decay of morals, pride, will to stay free.
So medieval Europe's life was blest,
By faith, the classics saved, brave chivalry.
Touched by despairing Anglo-Saxon slaves,
To make them "angels," rest of life he sought.
These caring words inscribed upon his tomb,
"To English Saxons Christian truth he taught."
Compassion, learning, Benedictine Rule,
Souls' music, life, the Church became the school.

*Hymn 146: "Now Let Us All With One Accord"*

# PATRICK

Sad day, yet hidden blessings, England's gift;

Young Patrick kidnapped, sold an Irish slave.

Long years as swineherd, time to care and pray,

Distressed for loving friends he longed to save.

God's Spirit called him, "Go now! Reach the coast."

An angel ship was there to rush him home!

What joy! What peace! Yet ease was soon to fade.

Lives touched by Christ are never more our own.

A vision message came; dream voices cried,

"Dear lad, come back and walk with us again."

He trained in Gaul; then sought lost friends of youth;

Poured out Christ's love in every hut and glen:

Saul's barn; proud Cashel's king; Armagh his See.

Lit Tara's Easter fire; still walks with me.

*Hymn 370: "I Bind Unto Myself Today*
*the Strong Name of the Trinity"*

*March 18*
*Bishop of Jerusalem, Great Teacher and Pastor*
*Died 386*

# CYRIL

The starving poor he tended, fed, relieved
With Church rich treasure, ornaments and gold;
When famine over, angry members cried:
"Illegal! Thief! Resign!" harsh voices cold.
Though driven out, his caring, loving won;
Restored, resumed great lessons for the Church:
Creed, Sacraments, Baptism, Holy Week.
Egeria, nun pilgrim, tells her search
For faith; and joy to hear this holy man.
When Arians compelled new sad exile,
Archbishop Theodosius bravely called
Him home; for none his love could long defile.
His catechism lives, in ours confessed:
Real Presence Eucharist, by Spirit blessed.

*Hymn 155: "All Glory, Laud and Honor to Thee,*
*Redeemer, King!"*

# ST. JOSEPH

God-fearing carpenter of Nazareth,
Betrothed to daughter of Joachim and Anne;
The Angel Gift of Glory Mary heard,
Would humbly come to her, as Heaven's Word.
The way to Bethlehem was long and wild,
Young mother, trem'lous, waiting for her child.
Protective Joseph watched the ancient road.
The patient donkey bore his precious load.
Faith grew that night of angels, shepherds, star;
Dream warned, the family fled to Egypt far,
'Til Spirit told, "No longer fear the kings!"
So God once more bore hope on "Eagle's wings."
Square, plane and saw helped shape young Jesus' soul.
Was God called "Father" for dear Joseph's role?

*Hymn 260: "Come Now, and Praise the Humble*
*Saint of David's House and Line"*

# CUTHBERT

In Britain's blessed Seventh Century
God called a man of love and piety.
From helpless lameness made a stranger whole.
His prayers saved boats of monks on storm-tossed sea.
Saw angels bearing Aidan's soul one night.
Gave Christ his life to tell of Heaven's light.
As Prior of Melrose sought the sick and poor;
Brought comfort, healing, hope, the Spirit's sight.
At Lindisfarne his thoughtful, patient way
Won Celtic monks to ancient Easter Day.
From cell on Farne, that lonely island rock,
Was called to shepherd wider loving flock.
Two years a caring Bishop, teacher, friend,
Then Angels called where Love will never end.

*Hymn 660: "O Master Let Me Walk With Thee"*

# THOMAS KEN

"Praise God from whom all blessings flow.
Praise Him all creatures here below.
Praise Him above ye heavenly hosts.
Praise Father, Son and Holy Ghost."
Hurt souls find peace in Ken's Doxology
Such faith helped him remain brave Anglican
When three kings failed to force him to their will.
Though banished from his see, stayed his own man!
Yet separated from his Church and King
Abhorring schism made peace with Queen Anne.
Great pastor, teacher, writer moving hymns
His will tells noble spirit of the man.
"I die in Apostolic Faith professed
Before disunion of the East and West."

*Hymn 43: "All Praise to Thee my God This Night"*

# JAMES DE KOVEN

He treasured Oxford Movement principles –
Devotion to the Sacraments and Creeds,
For others "live more nearly as we pray";
Expressive beauty worship meets deep needs.
But much of church opposed symbolic forms.
De Koven moved Convention with his plea,
"You take away our altars, incense lights –
We will submit," yet claim the mystery –
"Adore Christ's presence in the Eucharist
The privilege of every Christian heart."
He helped to keep the Church a family,
Not fearing change as each soul finds his part.
Helped keep the Church from faith rules, doctrinaire;
Urged open to the Spirit, "instant prayer."

*Hymn 318: "Here, O My Lord, I See Thee Face to Face"*

# GREGORY THE ILLUMINATOR

Young prince was rescued by his Christian nurse
From death at hands of father's enemies.
He grew to faith in Caesarean home;
Returned to teach and share God's mysteries.
Refused to sacrifice with pagan King;
Confined to pit for fourteen tortured years.
His sister's vision – King allowed release.
He preached and moved King Tiridate's tears.
With royal help he won this land to Christ;
Ordained as bishop, organized the Church.
With Gregory the King met Constantine;
Made pact of peace that spurred their Godly search.
His Mary bore two sons, their joy and pride;
One helped Nicea's faith be purified.

*Hymn 544: "Jesus Shall Reign Where-e'er the Sun"*

# THE ANNUNCIATION
# OF OUR LORD

The angel's "Hail," the maiden's trem'lous cry,
"Be unto me according to Thy will,"
Began a song of Heaven touching earth
That lifts our souls and raises visions still.
Oh dear melodious night beneath the stars
When Mary stroked the little Saviour's Head!—
Three years of pain and joy she strengthened, loved
'Til saw His glory, risen from the dead.
Her final gift was when the Lord looked down
To see His friends begin the great world search
For souls; and there His Mother, Brothers stood
Right in the center of His infant Church!
This Holy Motherhood, so awesome, sweet—
How many hearts and lives are more complete!

*Hymn 265: "The Angel Gabriel from Heaven Came"*

# CHARLES HENRY BRENT

First reached to thousands souls who knew not Christ:

The pagan Igorots of vast Luzon;

The hostile Sulu Moros felt his care,

Manila Chinese, Gospel brought new dawn.

He founded charity hospital, schools for poor.

He fought dread opium's so deadly blight,

Built friendship with the Independent Church;

Urged government be always fair, seek right.

One cherished cause was Christian unity;

He helped to call the first World Conference

On Faith and Order, held in Switzerland.

Whatever place he made a difference.

A man of prayer; whom children loved in play;

A saint of God, drove million tears away.

*Hymn 530: "Spread, O Spread Thou Mighty Word"*

*March 29.*
*Priest, Shepherd of the Oxford Movement*
*Died 1866*

# JOHN KEBLE

"New ev'ry morning is the love
Our wakening and uprising prove
Through sleep and darkness safely brought
Restored to life and power and thought." [1]
Great pastor sought to share his faith in God,
In daily services and visiting,
In confirmation classes, counseling.
Reached out to teachers, children, village schools.
He took defiant stand when Parliament
Revoked ten bishoprics in Ireland.
He preached on "National Apostocy,"
How morals fall when State rules over Church.
Led faith's return to deep devotion way;
Called all "to live more nearly as we pray." [2]

[1] The Christian Year, 1857. *The Hymnal 1982,*
   *No 10*
[2] *Ibid*

*Hymn 10: "New Every Morning Is the Love"*

# JOHN DONNE

"No man is an island" tells his life.
Carefree youth, then law and served the state.
World turmoil, conflict moved his caring heart
Ordained at last, gave Lord his life and fate.
The nation struggled, torn in throes of change.
Royal chaplain, rector, Dean of St. Paul's last.
His soul was moved by sense that all mankind
Are spirit linked, find God hands holding fast.
His preaching healed, made lives of many new.
Some made his plea for brotherhood their Call.
"His hand shall bind up all our scattered leaves
For that library open to us all."
"Any death diminishes" – still me.
"Ask not for whom the bell tolls – tolls for thee."

*Hymn 140: "Wilt Thou Forgive That Sin Where I Begun"*

# FREDERICK DENNISON MAURICE

Sad working class conditions of the poor;

Child labor where youth slept by their machines;

He called for radical non-violent reform

So every child could hope to live his dreams.

He taught love—faith in God who has redeemed –

"In whom I vindicate my rights as man."

We must engage in, sooner or later,

Unsocial Christians and unchristian socialists

Maurice saw worship as a source of strength,

Compassion, Church's mission, nobler mind.

"We are not (just) to praise the liturgy

But to use it" for the conscience of mankind.

Wage earners' college, Christian unity.

Such causes he inspired, what ministry!

*Hymn 542: "Christ Is the World's True Light"*

# JAMES LLOYD BRECK

Felt called to bring Christ's love to pioneers.

Nashotah House, Wisconsin wilderness

Brought struggling settlers witness of God's care.

Through study, work and prayer soul peace confessed.

In Minnesota sought the Indians;

Gull Lake, Columba's Mission, Chippewa.

New mission, Faribault, would point the way

For great Cathedral his dreams foresaw.

An educator blessed, he founded two

New seminaries for our Western Church.

Seabury and Nashotah, much we owe

To priests inspired there for souls to search.

Last gift five missions near Pacific Shore.

He fired Church 'gainst worldliness; seek more.

*Hymn 541: "Come Labor On"*

# RICHARD OF CHICHESTER

Young orphan, destitute, saved family home;

Restored its life, hard labor, gentle care.

At Oxford gave his all toward being ordained;

No gown, nor fire, yet faithful life of prayer.

Bologna, Paris, studied canon law.

Proud Canterbury named him Chancellor.

Elected Bishop of Chichester See

Made Henry Third in jealous rage deplore;

His choice rejected as incompetent.

So Richard banned from his cathedral home!

Two years on foot he sought out served his flock;

King reconciled at last, no need to roam.

Lived simply, teacher, pastor for his Lord;

Willed all to ill and poor; still love outpoured.

*Hymn 654: "Day by Day"*

# MARTIN LUTHER KING, JR.

Emancipation Proclamation freed
Sad people bound by prejudice and greed.
Yet "men created equal" still defied;
Cruel segregation. Founders' dreams denied,
'Til Rosa Parks kept bravely her bus seat
And thousands walked with Martin, fearless feet,
From Selma to Montgomery while glad world
Heard "We shall overcome," peace flag unfurled!
Marched black and white together, hand in hand,
As hope for fairness, justice filled the land.
Hard road to Washington, great call to dreams;
In Memphis martyred, yet love's light still gleams.
Thank you, O Christ, for Martin's caring gift;
May love and justice heal each human rift.

*Hymn 648: "When Israel Was in Egypt's Land, Let My People Go"*

# WILLIAM AUGUSTUS MUHLENBERG

Heard God call Church to live her Sacraments.

His boy's school trained church leaders twenty years.

Holy Communion Parish sought lost poor;

Blessed country trips, street children dried their tears;

Love fund for hungry, homeless, unemployed;

In weekly Eucharist Christ nourished all.

Helped Anne Ayres found Communion Sisterhood;

Helped found New York St. Luke's great Hospital.

Memorialized Convention: "Broader Church," —

More worship freedom, yet with catholic

Creeds, Eucharist, ordain historically;

Stressed Bible grace, save souls, reach lost, heal sick.

Like Godly music fills a church with glory

His caring love still moves our Church's story.

*Hymn 567: "Thine Arm O Lord, in Days of Old Was Strong
to Heal and Save"*

*April 9*
*Pastor, Theologian and Martyr in Germany*
*Like Jesus – a man for others. Died 1945*

# DIETRICH BONHOEFFER

When Nazis came to power, call began.

He sensed the awesome danger – faith and strife.

Led seminary for Confessing Church;

Wrote Life Together, discipline for life.

Cost of Discipleship: obedience

And faith mature two sides of one;

Faith moves obedience and Christ is met

When costly serving Him in everyone

World danger lectures in United States;

Brave heart returned to help Resistance fight.

Vast terror in his nation, took his stand;

His prison Letters promise of the light.

One last sweet April dawn at Flossenberg;

He knelt in prayer once more – and angels heard.

*Hymn 695: "By Gracious Power Is Wonderfully Sheltered"*

# WILLIAM LAW

"If we are to follow Christ, it must

Be in our common way – of every day"[1]

How like St. Paul, "I'm all things to all men,

So by all means save some." This Godly way [2]

Made Law a special priest, of many hearts'

Simplicity, devotion, charity.

Lives still in Carey's, Whitfield's, Wesley's gifts;

Revivals of the Eighteenth century.

As "non Juror" no State paid salary.

He worked as tutor, freelance minister;

He organized schools, homes for children poor;

'Gainst Deists, Sacraments and Scripture sure;

Condemned the ghastly warfare of his day;

How blessed for us to follow such life way!

[1] A Serious Call to a Devout and Holy Life
[2] *1st Corinthians 9:22*

*Hymn 707: "Take My Life and Let It Be Consecrated Lord to Thee"*

# GEORGE AUGUSTUS SELWYN

His heart was moved like Call Isaiah heard;

His, "Here am I, send me," led 'cross the world.

Two decades shared the love of Christ for all

In farthest place where British flag unfurled.

The Maoris and Colonists lived fear,

Expecting fierce revenge for cruelties;

Found bridge for peace to bless God's shepherd land

By his impartial caring ministries.

Both loved his patient listening concerns,

His pastoring of both their faults and needs.

Church Synod, Constitution gave new hope;

Now side by side they planted peace; best seeds.

Pacific Islands, too, preached Christ would save;

At Lichfield Maoris still seek his grave.

*Hymn 542: "Christ Is the World's True Light"*

# ALPHEGE

"From wrath of Northmen Lord deliver us."
So prayed the English Monks, brave faith affirmed.
When Bishop, Alphege won Olaf, Norse King;
Baptized, he made sweet peace and was confirmed.
When made beloved Archbishop, cared for all
Until next Norse invasion tore the land.
They forced him to their ships, abused and bound.
Enormous ransom raised; met their demand.
Yet he forbad his dear friends' burdened gift.
Moved Viking Captain tried to save dread strife;
By offering his all, except his ship.
Though anger won, love murdered won new life;
Now gentle martyr's witness not denied;
Touched by his care for them more were baptized!

*Hymn 595: "God of Grace and God of Glory"*

# ANSELM

Beloved of English People, caring, wise,

Fought long to keep the Church of England free.

No king invests Divine Authority;

In Call from Christ one's true appointment lies.

Two exiles hard 'til honored compromise:

His sacred mission blessed by Holy Church;

King's homage freed God's faithful, his soul's search;

This sharing or prophetic freedom dies.

He sought for reasoned faith in God Supreme

Whose love in Christ atones for all our sin.

His letters brought hurt lives encouragement;

From far he pastored, sought lost souls to win.

Returned, led Henry First make sad wrongs cease;

Bound up a wounded church with love and peace.

*Hymn 685: "Rock of Ages, Cleft for Me"*

# ST. GEORGE

Courageous Roman soldier gave his life
Upholding Christian virtue, noble strife.
At Lydda innocence of love was lost;
All saw what evil overcome might cost.
Through years his "slaying dragon" legend rose
To tell his dedication 'gainst Christ's foes.
He typifies brave soldiers through the years
Who gave their all to overcome world fears.
Jerusalem's Cathedral patron home;
Proud English named George patron saint their own.
In farthest lands the name, St. George, is raised
In memory brave hearts long honored, praised.
Oh may all wars their miseries now cease;
Christ, bring mankind your blessed, caring peace.

*Hymn 548: "Soldiers of Christ Arise"*

# ST. MARK

The first glad story of our Savior's life
Was told when young John Mark, bold Peter's scribe,
Preserved his martyr's witness, "Son of God!"
E're Simon too, head down, was crucified.
He saw and fled that night, the Lord's arrest;
Heard Peter's knock when prayer had set him free;
Then dared to preach with Barnabas and Paul
'Til lost his nerve beside the Syrian Sea.
Yet ministry in prison won Paul's heart.
Bold Peter spoke of him as, "Mark, my son."
His action Gospel breathes Christ's healing faith
And Cross of Love where life from death was won.
The Lion of St. Mark, what fitting sign!
Egyptian martyrdom, dear Venice shrine.

*Hymn 231: "For Mark, O Lord, We Praise You"*

# CATHERINE OF SIENA

A child was moved by vision of the Lord

In glory with Saint Peter, John and Paul.

The Savior smiled and blessed, transformed her soul;

Began her pilgrimage to heed His call.

Long years of fastings, prayers, temptations faced,

Through lonesome fears of God's abandonment,

She persevered, devout Dominican,

'Til Christ appeared with Mary, Heaven sent.

Then nursing worst in pain became her peace.

She labored through dread plagues, helped fears to cease;

Brought hope to sinners; cared for those condemned;

Urged rival Popes forgive, Christ's Body mend.

Her Dialogue poured out in ecstasy.

Her life of selfless love the ages see.

*Hymn 667: "Sometimes a Light Surprises"*

# ST. PHILIP & ST. JAMES

So many faithful faces round our Christ!
Some left us Bible books and martyrdoms.
Yet others then and midst our Christian struggles since
Were listeners, teachers, helpers — small days won.
When Philip brought Nathaniel to Christ.
A new Apostle born, "faith mustard seed."
When Jesus fed the seaside multitude
Calm Philip helped proclaiming people's need.
Last Supper Philip asked, "See Father God."
This searching question Jesus moves our tears,
"With you so long yet you do not know me?
See me and see the Father!" no more fears.
Young James who left no letters just his love
Watched fearlessly at cross, points Heaven above.

*Hymn 233: "The Eternal Gifts of Christ the King"*

# ATHANASIUS

From youth he fought to keep man's greatest gift:
True faith in Christ as God before all time.
Creator came Himself in Mary's womb,
To cleanse, transform, restore souls to Divine.
No holy saint could lift our race from sin.
God-Man alone reclaimed His image lost.
Nicaea's Council blessed this Christian core,
Which Athanasius led at fearful cost.
The Arians denied one Father-Son.
Three times they drove the Bishop from his See.
From Egypt's hermit caves and refuge Rome
He counseled, wrote and taught the Trinity.
Restored, exiled twice more, he won the day;
His martyr's life helped save the Christian Way.

*Hymn 423: "Immortal, Invisible God Only Wise"*

# MONNICA

A godly home, devoted servant's care;
She safely came through subtle trials of youth.
Her patience won a faithless husband's heart;
Her prayers led him, baptized, to new life start.
Love pleas persisted for her troubled son
Whose brilliant mind forsook first Scripture trust.
Soul starved by mans' philosophies and sin,
He found at last her Christ who calls within.
From Africa she'd followed to Milan.
What joy to see him kneeling by her side!
What peace! Gone vigil nights of prayerful tears.
Dear mother, wife, what model through the years!
Oh Monnica, God blesses still your prayer;
Our Christian world made nobler, wiser there.

*Hymn 662: "Abide With Me"*

# DAME JULIAN
# OF NORWICH

Three gifts she sought: Christ's passion understood;
Her pain to fathom His; three wounds to bear:
Heart felt contrition, deep compassion's soul,
Divine God-longing, all her life to share.
At thirty, gravely ill, received last rites;
On seventh day pain left amazingly.
Then fifteen "showings" of His Cross of Love
Brought holy peace and joy eternally.
In solitude, her Savior's Anchoress,
She learned His meaning was this deepest love.
As counselor she showed "Our Courteous Lord"
To all who longed to know the life above.
He said to her, for us, "all shall be well;
I can make, will make, shall make all things well."

*Hymn 487: "Come My Way, My Truth, My Life"*

# GREGORY OF NAZIANZUS

A bishop's son found light in Athens' soul;

With dear friend, Basil, sought a life more whole.

Monastic rest on Pontus brought true peace;

Their witness for Christ's love would never cease.

His father called him home to be ordained;

Unworthy felt, yet noble priesthood claimed.

As bishop preached Christ, Savior, gift for all;

Then answered torn Constantinople's call.

House-Church, alone, to Orthodox was left;

His faith renewed a city, hope bereft.

His message shared One God, the Trinity,

The Cross that heals, redeems and sets us free.

He led the Eastern Church, new life, restored;

His pastorate proclaimed the Living Lord.

*Hymn 473: "Lift High the Cross"*

# DUNSTAN

Defense against invasions, tribal wars
Brought British faith, morale to near despair;
'Til Spirit-touched young monk felt call to bring
To Glastonberry Benedictine care.
Blest Rule revived that monastery's life;
Scriptorium responded; hearts were fed.
Example spread throughout a weary land.
From Abbot to Archbishop Dunstan led.
For people mostly steeped in arts of war
New peace, new trust, new Christian virtue came;
Schools, farms, shops, monasteries reappeared.
Loose morals, slavery began to wane.
His special gift was music for the soul.
His life remembered still makes ours more whole.

*Hymn 564: "He Who Would Valiant Be 'gainst All Disaster"*

# ALCUIN

What heritage inspired special gifts! –
Related to the noble Willibrord,
First missionary to the Netherlands.
In York's Cathedral School he found his Lord;
Archbishop Egbert there moved his young heart
With faith learned from the Venerable Bede.
In Italy's blessed ancient Pavia,
Where rests the tomb of honored Augustine,
He met with Charlemange, the Great, of France
Who made him education head of all his realm.
St. Martin's Monastery's life at Tours
Revived with him as Abbot at its helm.
His schools, libraries saved rich classic past.
New liturgies helped Christian treasures last.

*Hymn 631: "Book of Books, Our People's Strength"*

# JACKSON KEMPER

Sent Indiana rough, Missouri wild;

One church in each; make these a power base.

Taught, served, loved, brought saving Christian hope.

Then these reached out: more souls now saw Christ's face.

So two dynamic diocese were born

He led new faith foundation Iowa,

Nebraska, Minnesota, Kansas hearts;

And reached first natives of America.

Nashotah House for clergy training, dream

Fulfilled to deepen worship, strengthen prayer.

"Let us rejoice in sending name of Lord

To those who cry, 'Come over help us bear.'"

"Love your own spiritual children" now.

"Close not your hearts to neighbor's anguished brow."[1]

[1] *Triennial Sermon before the Board of Missions*
*1841 Quoted in* They Still Speak.
*J. Robert Wright, Church Pension Fund, 1993*

*Hymn 719: "O Beautiful for Spacious Skies"*

# BEDE, THE VENERABLE

The Seventh Century, that Golden Age

Of Lindesfarne, proud Canterbury, Rome

Was saved for all our British heritage

By Bede who called St. Paul's of Jarrow home.

His History of saints and martyrs glows

With courage, trust and love that moves us still.

His gracious just discernment tells our souls

How God heals lives, His purpose to fulfill.

Bede's faith helped Alfred mend torn England's heart;

Sent Alcuin to lead reforms in Gaul.

Like gleam of blue that grows between dark clouds,

Bede's wisdom spread Christ light wide over all.

Devoted monk who loved his Daily Hours;

Such caring lives as his are nations' flowers.

*Hymn 217: "A Hymn of Glory Let Us Sing"*

# AUGUSTINE

King Ethelbert received St. Augustine

Moved by Queen Bertha's prayerful Christian life.

He welcomed forty monks Pope Gregory

Had sent to preach God's love, save human strife.

A silver cross and picture of our Lord

They carried to new Canterbury home.

St. Martin's, oldest church from Roman days,

Where Bertha worshipped, now they made their own.

Pure holy lives of service, prayer and peace

Won converts to the Lord, each searching heart.

King Ethelbert himself was won, baptized;

His subjects followed; English church fresh start.

Pope said seek best in Churches everywhere;

Diversity with unity born there.

*Hymn 691: "My Faith Looks Up to Thee"*

# THE VISITATION

She sought hill county, dear Elizabeth
To share with cousin her own special joy;
Blest Gabriel brought promise glorious;
She would bring forth for world God's holy boy.
Elizabeth hailed Mary with the words,
"Blessed are you blest fruit of your womb."
Then Mary's joy sang forth "Magnificat";
And unborn John, leaped for such joy to bloom.
He sensed his mission to proclaim the Lord,
Whose coming later to all Israel
Would break the bonds of sin, declare new hope;
Christ's mercy, healing, saving love to tell.
O precious moment for each gentle girl!
O blessed moment for a searching world!

*Hymn 269: "Ye Who Caim the Faith of Jesus"*

*June 1*
*Early Christian Apologist, Martyr at Rome*
*Died C. 167*

# JUSTIN

Born near old Jacob's Well; long sought, adored
The "Living Water" promised by his Lord.
In Stoics' virtue, Pythogoras's freed soul,
In Plato's conscience strove to find life whole.
Still restless, walked the beach at Ephesus
'Til stranger told of Christ's gifts glorious.
"Straightway a flame was kindled in my soul,"
He wrote; and gave his life to Christ, his goal.
He built a school in Rome of loving zeal;
Taught caring God who human ills would heal;
Trust reasoned faith, be loyal to the State;
Charged Cynics' school corrupt, in fierce debate.
Condemned as atheist, clung to his Lord;
With six dear students perished by the sword.

*Hymn 238: "Blessed Hearts of Blessed Martyrs"*

# THE MARTYRS OF LYONS

Condemned for atheism, blasphemy,
Perversion, treason, enemies of gods;
Wild public trials to please the Emperor;
Imprisoned, tortured, bodies thrown to dogs.
Physician, Alexander, asked God's name;
"God has no name as men have," brave reply;
"You pagans are the ones men's flesh consume,"
He charged them, as in fire prepared to die.
Pothinus, Bishop; Deacon, Sanctus, killed;
With beaten Ponticus, just fifteenth year.
Attalus, notable, took Christ's hard path.
Blandina, slave, cried, "Nothing wicked here."
The "Well of Martyrs" is their shrine today
By hallowed Rhone, in church, St. Irenee.

*Hymn 552: "Fight the Good Fight With All Thy Might"*

# THE MARTYRS OF UGANDA

When Anglicans and Roman Catholics

Together brought the Faith, were well received.

Mutesa, King, approved their caring lives,

The change Christ brought to those who first believed.

Then Mwanga, Animistic, took the throne.

Was angered that some loved a higher king,

Banned missions; then all Christians' lives he sought.

Three youths burned first; yet through the flames would ring,

"We daily, daily sing Thy praises, Lord."

Then thirty-two court pages tortured, burned;

Sang love while died at Namugongo's fires.

Moved souls now sought such faith. God's tide was turned!

We pray beside these brothers, sisters still.

Our dreams, our trust, our peace, His larger Will.

*Hymn 545: "Lo! What a Cloud of Witnesses"*

# THE FIRST BOOK OF COMMON PRAYER

The format, substance, style primarily
Soul work of Thomas Cranmer for his day.
He used wide sources for his godly themes;
Past centuries would still lift hearts to pray.
Latin service books of Sarum use;
Gallican and rich Greek liturgy;
Luther's German forms vernacular:
"Great Bible" English, early Litany,
Were sources proven long for spirit life.
It simplified the worship of the Church.
Both clergy, laity found living strength;
For joy, peace, comforting it helped their search;
Supports us all through every daily strife;
It binds us all in caring giving life.

*Hymn 8: "Morning Has Broken"*

# BONIFACE

An English monk, returning Europe's gift,
Brought Christ to dread Friesland, wild Saxony.
As Bishop, from Thor's sacred oak cut down
Built Peter's church to set awed pagans free.
Archbishop, Primate of vast German lands,
Paul's "care of all the churches" felt his love.
Conferred with kings; revived despoiled French Church;
Yet still heard call to mission from Above.
When seventy-five tried rough Friesland again.
Whitsunday Eve, vast confirmations due;
When savage warriors struck him down he cried,
"Return not evil; trust that God loves you."
In Fulda by dear cousin, abbess, lies;
Called Boniface; God's light through his brave eyes.

*Hymn 525: "The Church's One Foundation Is Jesus Christ Her Lord"*

# COLUMBA

Soft grasses blowing o'er primeval rocks,

White lambs like jewels on gentle slopes serene,

Iona, Isle of Spirit, found her own

When humbled sad Columba crossed the sea.

'Tis said deep hurts of conscience drove him far,

Beloved Ireland to see no more,

Until three thousand souls replaced those lost

Because his pride allowed a dread clan war.

Community of work and prayer was born

Whose love reached out to win dear Scotland's heart;

And ever since, his haven pilgrims seek

For mystic oneness, God within, to start.

St. Martin's Celtic Cross still guards his cell.

His Hill of Angels whispers, "All is well."

*Hymn 645: "The King of Love My Shepherd Is"*

*June 10*
*Deacon, Syrian Doctor of the Church, and Poet*
*Died 373*

# EPHREM OF EDESSA

"Lord, shed upon our darkened souls your light,

Your Holy wisdom for our daily strife;

In Sacrament we rest in your embrace.

Grant that we come to know the risen life.

We glimpse the beauty you laid up for us

When gazing on the beauty of your will.

Lord, may we haste to our true city home

Like Moses on the mountain saw it still." [1]

From cave retreat poured forth a spirit flood,

Hymns, prayers, defining works of Gospel Love.

He brought the sick and poor Christ's tender care;

He formed a school to lift men's thoughts above.

"None saw, has seen, what you have seen," he said

"The Lord, Himself, is altar, priest and bread."

[1] *From Sermon quoted in* They Still Speak
*by J. Robert Wright, 1993, Church Hymnal
Corporation.*

*Hymn 443: "From God Christ's Deity Came Forth"*

# ST. BARNABAS

From Cyprus reached Jerusalem found Christ.

Since Pentecost Apostle's spirit power

Brought many hearts to resurrection faith;

So Barnabas life-changed in destined hour.

Inspired, sold field, gave Apostles all.

He vouched for Paul's conversion to the church;

Sought him to help Christ's mission Antioch

Which sent them to Galatia, new souls search.

Returning won acceptance faith alone

Finds God without rules man-made faithless loss.

Young Mark he took to Cyprus, founded church.

He traveled far to share Christ's saving Cross.

Was called Encourager for he would see

And help dear others in their ministry.

*Hymn 231: "For Barnabas We Praise You"*

# ENMEGAHBOWH

From Canada as missionary sought
To bring Christ's love to Ojibways his goal.
Discouraged, he began return; great storm
On Lake Superior foretold his role.
As ship held back by gale his vision seen
"At Nineveh scared Jonah saying 'no'
Refused to preach there fled to Tarshish dream."
Now, Enmegahbowh went where God said "Go."
At Gull Lake built church, St. Columba's, there.
Ordained a deacon then a priest, he won
More deacons for new lives of prayerful care;
Thru Minnesota taught, "In Christ be one."
Ojibways learned to sing God's hymns of glory;
Their Christian music telling Jesus' story.

*Hymn 385: "Many and Great, O God, Are Thy Works"*

# BASIL THE GREAT

When Nicene Creed was under dread attack,

And State joined those who Christ divine denied,

Proud grandson of a martyr joined the fray;

God called a saint to stem the Arian tide.

Dear sister led his brilliance to the Lord;

In cloistered path, he felt faith's love increase;

By sister's river convent built his cell;

As "patriarch" of monks, taught caring peace.

Constantinople's council witnessed bold;

When Caesarea's Bishop, cared for all;

Whole suburb built for healing sick and poor;

'Til even foes praised one who stood so tall.

Exhausted. Died to save the Trinity;

Great mind, great soul, kept faith for you and me.

*Hymn 363: "Ancient of Days"*

# EVELYN UNDERHILL

Through all of Christian history mystics came,

Soul-sensitive they helped us feel God near;

Calm Benedict; Augustine humble; Francis' love;

Dame Julian's visions, "all is well" so dear.

Our Anglican awakening renewed

When Evelyn explored faith's mystic source;

Taught adoration vital spring of prayer;

Led others down same spirit rivers' course.

Her writing's lead our thoughts Christ's saving Way:

"The fact of prayer is the "law of belief"":

"Response is worship 'til Eternal Day";

"The Origin, Sustainer and the End."

For mysticism pierces doubt and gloom

With guiding light so hope and life can bloom.

*Hymn 503: "Come Holy Ghost, Our Souls Inspire"*

# JOSEPH BUTLER

The church was torn in Eighteenth Century,
The Deists taught one God alone Divine;
Some Evangelicals were thought to be
Too far from reason's ancient honored time.
Within traditions Apostolic Church,
God, Savior, Holy Spirit, three in One;
He led his people's hearts in eager search
In Scriptures, Prayers for Jesus, Holy Son.
Great pastor served the mind as well as soul,
Warm caring life, society concern
Endeared him to his flock, his faith their goal,
They sought his life of prayer, Christ's way to learn.
So Joseph Butler and the Wesleys gave
Their hearts and minds dear England's faith to save.

*Hymn 362: "Holy, Holy, Holy"*

# BERNARD MIZEKI

When early teen sought freedom, peace, new hope;

Fled fierce oppression, grim East Africa;

Escaped to Cape Town refuge with the Church;

Found Bible faith, the joy of Christian love.

Baptized, he served in wild Mashonaland;

At Nhowa taught the Gospel, trust in prayer;

Freed lives from superstition, ignorance.

Five years he brought Christ's healing loving care.

When native pride and culture felt ignored,

In foreigners saw power hungry greed,

Bernard was warned to flee a dangerous land.

He chose to stay, support dear friends in need.

When killed defending converts' Christian goals,

He joined long centuries of martyred souls.

*Hymn 356: "May Choirs of Angels Lead You to Paradise on High"*

# ALBAN

"Arrest the traitor Christians!" soldiers cried.

While scouring grimly old Verulamium.

A priest in fear of death reached Alban's door;

He risked his life to take condemned one in.

The fugitive was worthy of his host;

Compassion grew to faith each passing hour.

Brave Alban met house-search in priest's long coat;

Implored his friend to live, to share Christ's power.

Arrested, judge demanded race and name:

"I'm now a Christian, bound by Jesus' will;

Called 'Alban,' true and living God adore."

Faith took him 'cross the valley, up the hill.

On flowered summit love had final say;

The best of England blossomed that hard day.

*Hymn 357: "Jesus, Son of Mary, Fount of Life Alone"*

# NATIVITY OF JOHN THE BAPTIST

When Zechariah doubted Gabriel
Elizabeth bore their prophetic son.
When Mary came to share maternal joy
She sang "Magnificat"; their hearts were one.
At Jordan's blessed stream John faced the crowd.
"Repent ye for the Kingdom is at hand."
Vast searching throngs came, humble, penitent;
Baptized, soul cleansed, pledged lives to God's demand.
When Jesus came dear cousin cried "Behold
The Lamb of God who takes away world's sin."
When Spirit came from Heaven as a dove,
A Voice, "Behold Beloved Son, Hear Him."
John martyred for brave call to purity.
Christ said, "No greater man will ever be."

*Hymn 76: On Jordan's Bank the Baptist's Cry"*

# IRENAEUS

A lad at feet of sainted Polycarp

Whose faith came pure from Lord's Beloved John, [1]

While still a youth, felt called to far Lyon

To share God's love beside the beauteous Rhone:

The World, our lives are spent and raised with Christ;

In Eucharist we see, like eyes divine,

Creation as Our Maker meant to be;

Apostles' truth, the Church's trust sets free.

While witnessing in Rome the dread news came,

Pothinus, aged Bishop, beaten, slain;

Blandina, other dear ones, gored and dead.

Doubt not he grieved, "Wouldst Thou took me instead."

The martyr's flock called him for Shepherd then,

First theologian for all Christian men.

[1] *Irenaeus,* Against Heresies, *Bk. III, Chapter 3*

*Hymn 363: "Ancient of Days"*

# ST. PETER & ST. PAUL

These two great leaders of the early church
Were martyred under Nero, sixty four.
Well educated, traveled, Jewish Paul,
Strong Peter called from Galilee's seashore.
About the Gentile mission disagreed;
Yet gospel faith outweighed thoughts of their own.
Paul killed with sword and Peter crucified;
They gave their lives for Christ in tortured Rome.
Wise Clement wrote to Corinth, "Let us come
To these who recently proved champions":
Brave Peter who endured hard painful trials;
Paul, seven times imprisoned, faithful ones.
Blest Peter witnessed Resurrection Day;
Blest Paul preached East and West the Christian Way.

*Hymn 273: "Two Stalwart Trees Both Rooted in Faith and Holy Love"*

# INDEPENDENCE DAY

Brave hearts on Christmas who crossed the Delaware;
Brought Washington to so fair Trenton Town.
Brave news at dawn on Christmas Day;
Some twenty thousand foes their arms laid down!
So dreams of freedom Bunker Hill not lost.
Conquered, Lexington revealed the cost.
Long way to Yorktown freedom came at last.
Oh Layfayette, praise God, you held us fast!
New cities west were promises of life;
'Neath noble thirteen bars and flag of stars.
Forget not, dear America of peace
That only wars of spirit help to cease.
Oh worship, worship God supreme above
Who gave us justice, mercy, humble caring love.

*Hymn 717: "My Country 'Tis of Thee"*

# BENEDICT OF NURSIA

The Fall of Rome made chaos in the West.
Some gave up principles in sad despair.
Some hid as hermits from a troubled world.
Young Benedict shared loving faith and prayer.
Withdrawing to Subiaco's rough cave,
He won disciples seeking Christ and peace.
Monte Cassino, next monastic home,
Proclaimed his Rule; and blessings never ceased.
Its balanced day of prayer, work, reading, rest
Saved Europe's soul with islands of Christ's love.
Augustine brought this Light to England's heart;
Her Boniface moved German thoughts Above.
How much of Christian culture saved with care!
How many lives were changed, discipled there!

*Hymn 482: "Lord of All Hopefulness"*

*July 17*
*Bishop of Pennsylvania, First presiding Bishop of the American Church*
*Died 1836*

# WILLIAM WHITE

Helped save the Church through Revolution's War
When Anglicans were seen allied with Kings;
Served Continental Congress, Chaplain proud;
Heard liberty's Great Bell's impassioned rings.
Chief architect of independent church,
First Bishop consecrated English Line.
Brought Apostolic Faith, a Shepherd's care;
In troubled darkened lives Christ's light would shine.
Led medical relief for indigents;
State Institute to aid the deaf and mute;
His city's conscience to cruel prison life,
First Sunday School by Anglicans took root.
Like Dunstan, Wulfstan, Hugh, before him, called,
"Loved Justice, Mercy, Humbly walked with God." [1]

[1] *Micah 6:8*

*Hymn 403: "Let All the World in Every Corner Sing"*

*July 19*
*Unnoticed saints are often nurturers of greatness in others:*
*Brothers – St. Basil the Great of Caesares, St. Gregory of Nyssa*
*Died 379*

# MACRINA

A beautiful young girl bethrothed at twelve;

Fiancé died; a single life she chose

More fully to serve Christ in others' lives.

She led her family to faith repose.

From model Christian home her parents gave

She sought to show hurt souls love paths untrod.

Through her the Spirit touched her brother proud;

'Til Basil changed his life, shared gifts for God.

She comforted her mother's loss of son;

Together formed community of nuns.

When Basil died, she followed deathly ill.

In arms of Gregory, her heaven won.

She prayed, "From fear of death you make us free;

Pray send a shining angel to lead me." [1]

[1] Voices of the Saints. *Bert Ghezzi, 2000*

*Hymn 610: "Lord, Whose Love Through Humble*
*Service Bore the Weight of Human Need"*

# ELIZABETH CADY STANTON

Hard doctrines hurt the faith of brave young life,
Predestination, man's depravity.
Depression healed by action, righting wrongs
On women by Church and society.
Said Church used Scripture to subordinate
In marriage and prohibit ministry.
Said World denied professions, right to vote,
Less pay same work, forbad owned property.
She preached in churches, dared in politics.
She brought a holy presence, reached irate.
Wrote Susan Anthony, "Dear friend faint not;
We suffer not in vain; we liberate."
At death wished she had more fulfilled her role
"Been braver, bolder, truer to my soul."

*Hymn 616: "Hail to the Lord's Annointed"*

# AMELIA JENKS BLOOMER

First woman editor of newspaper;
Her Lily voiced sad cries, female despair;
How liquor tore hurt families apart;
Trapped women lost in stifled lives unfair.
Of St. Paul's views she said, "Could he have looked
Into the future and forseen the strife,
Oppression cringing fear submission" caused
By well meant words for his days, woman's life,
"He never would have uttered them." Of rights
To freedom, "The same power that brought the slave
From bondage will in good time bring about
Emancipation, womens' dreams to save."
Her bloomers worn freed others', skirts of pain;
Helped Church, libraries, schools — her gifts remain.

*Hymn 602: "Jesu, Jesu"*

# ISABELLA (SOJOURNER TRUTH)

An angel warrior – God's children lost,
Fled slavery with help of Quaker friends.
Evangelist, street corners of New York.
Brought women homeless shelter; torn life mends;
Good food, warm clothing, caring gave fresh start.
When asked her name, "My name is Sojourner."
"Last name" She thought all her slave masters' names.
"The Master I have now is God. His name is Truth."
As travelling preacher pleaded women's rights.
Moved hearts to feel the pain of slavery.
"Ain't I a woman" speech made people think
Of Christ's example, women He set free.
Her charismatic presence breathed God's love.
Taught equal care for all, our Home above.

*Hymn 615: "Thy Kingdom Come"*

# HARRIET ROSS TUBMAN

To freedom led three hundred slaves oppressed
Like Moses with Egyptian hosts behind
And Red Sea waters looming wall ahead.
Faith "Underground Railway" new lives would find.
Her nineteen trips were perilously brave;
Full forty thousand pledged for her arrest.
Rough wagon rides 'neath sacks to Quaker homes;
Long days, hard nights fled North to peace and rest.
In Civil War was soldier, spy and nurse.
She cared for wounded, both sides, fearlessly.
War over built home, orphans, elderly;
Joined fight for women's rights and dignity.
A Liberty Ship's name; own postage stamps
Reflect her caring, lighting freedom's lamps.

*Hymn 527: "Singing Songs of Expectation"*

*July 22*
*A Disciple of the Lord from Magdala*
*Apostle to the Apostles in Eastern Church*

# ST. MARY MAGDALENE

Her life was changed forever by her Lord;
Thought lost beyond redemption, saved by grace.
Her Galilean village, honored name
Because she saw the Glory in His Face.
She witnessed in His early teaching days
By serving Him and His disciples there.
She stood by His dear Mother at the Cross;
Watched Nicodemus, Joseph's last kind care.
Soft Easter dawn, strange empty tomb, despair;
"They've taken 'way my Lord I know not where"
Then, "Mary!" "Master!" Joy! Reached out, adored!
He sent her back to tell, "I've seen the Lord!"
What comfort to us who have often erred
That Mary heard His first glad Easter word!

*Hymn 232: "All Praise for Mary Magdelene"*

# THOMAS À KEMPIS

His Imitation calls us to our Christ;
The Grace of God alone can make us whole.
Temptations fade; humility brings peace;
Serving, loving lift a lonely soul.
Some progress in self-conquest leads us on.
Pure heart and simple purpose are more sure.
Jesus' friendship lights our upward path;
His Cross is ours; His life helps us endure.
Though worldly perils haunt our steep ascent,
Still looms far off the glorious Mount divine.
At last embraced within your saving arms;
Surrendered, faith filled, we are wholly thine.
Some years remain before our Heavenly Home;
Yet at your Table, we are now your own.

*Hymn 488: "Be Thou My Vision"*

# ST. JAMES

Such heavy nets to mend! Then blessed pause.
Friends Andrew, Peter; Rabbi with life call;
"Come follow me and you will fish for men."
Young James and John hearts moved, souls touched, left all.
"Sons of Thunder: called, impetuous.
Rest angered when they asked for seats beside
The Lord; then patient caring Jesus taught,
"Who would be first must serve you all," not pride.
He sensed in these two brothers spirit depth;
Brought them to see Transfiguration Light;
Prayed close with them in soul wrenched agony
Beneath the olive trees that tragic night.
James lived to share Christ's glory Easter-tide;
Then first Apostle killed, reached Master's side.

*Hymn 232: "O Lord, for James We Praise You"*

# ANNE & JOACHIM

How blessed were the parents of this child!
Tradition places Anne in David's Line,
A Hebrew family devout with hope
For long dreamed Messianic sign.
When Mary came, a sweet and trusting child,
They nurtured her with prayerful guiding care.
Then graceful home skills, Rabbi school, dear friends.
Brought water from the village well, dreamed there,
While watching peaceful life of Nazareth,
Of vague strange awesome challenges ahead.
Her manly father modeled holy life.
Her gentle mother led prayers by her bed.
Such home prepared glad answer Angel heard,
"Be unto me according to Thy Word"

*Hymn 708: "Savior Like a Shepherd Lead Us"*

# WILLIAM REED HUNTINGTON

The Ancient Deaconesses were revived;
His parish, Grace, New York, where women trained.
Revision of the prayer Book Ninety Two,
More worship flexible, faith care remained.
The passion of his life, church unity;
Said Anglican base principles can bring;
All Christians closer to their Lord as One;
Can heal fraternal wounds before our King.
"The Holy Scriptures as the Word of God;
The Primitive creeds as the Rule of Faith;
Two Sacraments ordained by Christ Himself;
Episcopate as Keystone Unity";
Would bring the church of Christ to sympathy
With throbbing, sorrowing hearts – Society.[1]

[1] *"Chicago – Lambeth Quadrilateral" for bringing Christians together in faith and stronger healing influence 1886 Chicago General Convention, 1888 Lambeth Conference in* They Still Speak, *J. Robert Wright, 1993.*

*Hymn 525: "The Church's One Foundation Is Jesus Christ Her Lord"*

# MARY & MARTHA OF BETHANY

Two sisters Jesus treasured, special friends;

Beloved Mount of Olives, their dear home,

His resting place of peace on journeys hard,

A refuge last dread week to call His own.

When Mary washed His feet with costly oil,

The Lord defended, "My Memorial."

While Mary worshipped, weary Martha served;

He said, "Let be; she chose best way of all."

When Jesus came too late for Lazarus,

Heard Martha's faith, "With you he'd not have died";

He said, "I am the Resurrection Life!

Do you believe ?" "Yes, Christ!" Yet Jesus cried.

Then, "Lazarus, come forth!" rings down the years

With awesome love to dry our human tears.

*Hymn 658: "As Longs the Deer for Cooling Streams"*

# WILLIAM WILBERFORCE

As lighthouse flashes safety cross cruel waves

He sought for all safe homes on British shore.

Aghast that slaves were captured, tortured, sold,

Felt call to priesthood, save and comfort more.

Repentant slaver wrote "Amazing Grace"

John Newton urged, "Do more in Parliament."

For fifty years he pled their human rights;

Save broken lives, lost loves, sad families rent

No more leg chained for weeks in dank ship holds;

No more exhausted deaths as last cries cease.

Humane full freedom voted Thirty Three.

Though gone a month his soul could rest in peace.

He warned, teach love and morals, educate,

"Let us beware before it is too late."

*Hymn 528: "Lord, You Give the Great Commission"*

# IGNATIUS OF LOYOLA

"He was a man for vanities of world.

Special delight in exercise of arms

With great and vain desire of glory won." [1]

Heroic act, grave wound, gave soul alarms.

His searching heart one night saw Love Divine,

The Virgin and her Son; this changed his life.

No more for glory seeking, carnal thoughts;

Placed sword on Lady altar, end of strife.

His Spiritual Exercises moved

The souls of others longing for their God;

They served the poor and shared their poverty;

Their caring lives won others, humbled, awed.

Society of Jesus reached the world;

They lifted high the Cross, Christ's love unfurled.

[1] *From his autobiography quoted in* Lesser Feasts
   and Fasts *2000, Episcopal Church p. 312*

*Hymn 707: "Take My Life and Let It Be Consecrated Lord to Thee"*

# JOSEPH OF ARIMATHEA

It was that grim foreboding midnight hour
When the Sanhedrin tried the Lord of life,
A tide that he and Nicodemus could not stem,
Ignored His mercies – words to end men's strife.
The jeering crowds, that cross so terrible
They watched until His last forgiving cry.
Then Joseph begged the body of his friend
And troubled Pilate nodded with a sigh.
They wrapped and spiced Him gently carefully;
In Joseph's own new tomb the Savior lay;
They spoke to grieving Marys watching near;
Then heavy hearted went their weary way.
When Easter came kind Joseph filled with glory;
Some say reached England with the wondrous story!

*Hymn 448: "O Love, How Deep, How Broad, How High"*

# OSWALD

When Aefelfrith, Destroyer, was the King,

Northumbria wild pagan land again;

For safety sent his children Sacred Isle,

Iona, in the care of holy men.

We wonder if he sought their better life,

For Oswald, son, met Sainted Aidan there.

Succeeding to his father's violent throne,

He called this gentle monk to heal despair;

Then walked beside him through sad troubled land;

Translated his love message, fed the weak;

Compassion, piety and learning shared;

Helped lead men toward the God all hearts will seek.

Gave life to save his people tragic loss;

Died fighting pagan warriors 'neath the Cross.

*Hymn 238: Blessed Feasts of Blessed Martyrs"*

# THE TRANSFIGURATION

From top this holy peak you saw the struggling world
Which heard your precious name at last unfurled,
Now "This beloved son of mine, hear him."
He looked again across sad land so dim.
The father's love shown through all glistening white.
Knelt Peter, John in awe at such a sight
Felt sweet and solemn mystery of such light
Felt power to build a world of truth and right.
Said Peter, "Build three altars"; times so wild.
Then down the mount they went healed hurting child.
They shared God's love in healing little one —
Back to that mount we look for help from Son.
With power from His sacramental meal
How many tired hearts new life here feel.

*Hymn 130: "Christ Upon the Mountain Peak"*

# JOHN MASON NEALE

In Church of England and America.
A gentle, modest, patient scholar priest,
Taught medieval heritage, rich, deep.
His forty Hymnal gifts still lift our hearts;
Faith music echoes cause soul thoughts to keep.
"Good Christian Men Rejoice," for Christmas Day;
"All Glory Laud and Honor," Sunday Palms;
"Come Ye Faithful Raise the Strain," for empty tomb;
"Christ Is Made the True Foundation," Heaven's balms.
Translating Greek and Latin hymns, he linked
Past to today. Our Prayer Book cites
"Sing, My Tongue, the Glorious Battle" for
Good Friday's liturgy climatic rites.
He founded Sisterhood St. Margaret for
Relief of women, girls, a saving door.

*Hymn 107: "Good Christian Friends Rejoice"*

*August 8*
*Priest and Friar, Founder of Dominican Friars – Preachers*
*Orthodox Reformer in the Middle Ages, Canon of Osma Cathedral,*
*Spain, Prior of the Community. Died 1221*

# DOMINIC

Sought Apostolic poverty, sold all

His goods to help the poor in famine grave.

Albigensians' sad heresy spread far.

He led trained preachers, share true faith and save.

These Dualists despised this "evil world";

Ignored the Incarnation, God in man.

He founded Preaching Order to maintain

God made all, loves all, cares, redeems, no ban.

His friars spread through Western Europe, peace;

Brought Medieval Church new trust, faith bloom:

Thomas Aquinas, "Teacher to the Church";

Michaelangelo who carved his tomb.

His love of God, joy filled, shone on his face;

Made Him strong bearer of Christ's saving grace.

*Hymn 644: "How Sweet the Name of Jesus Sounds*
*in a Beliver's Ear!"*

# LAURENCE

He brought Christ's love to troubled, helpless, weak

When Emperor Valerian had jailed

Rome's Bishop, Sixtus, and attacked the church

But never grasped why persecutions failed.

Valerian sought Christian treasury;

Arrested Laurence who was left in charge,

Not knowing he with tender pastor's care

Had fed and nurtured city's poor at large!

Forced to comply he called great homeless crowd;

Cries proudly "Those are the Church's treasures now."

The court condemned him who held faith so dear

To slowly roast on flamed grid iron bier.

Upon the shoulders of such dauntless love

We stand, share faith and trust for Life above.

*Hymn 194: "Jesus Lives! Thy Terrors Now Can*
*No Longer, Death, Appall Us"*

# CLARE OF ASSISI

Moved by the teaching of St. Francis' love,

When eighteen joined the Benedictine nuns.

Her sister, then her widowed mother came;

With Francis' help they formed the first "Poor Clares";

Superior of convent forty years.

They followed same strict rules of poverty,

Humility, devotion, serving poor;

By begging fed them, nursed them, dried their tears,

Told Francis, "I am yours. Give will to God."

So radiated spirit, power strong,

"She kindled those who only heard her name."

Last illness dear friends came; her faith still awed.

On her last day said, "Go in peace, no fear."

"He who created you, loves you, stays near."

*Hymn 593: "Lord, Make Us Servants of Your Peace"*

# FLORENCE NIGHTINGALE

"'Tis lady with the lamp," calmed whispers spread,

As through the suffering wards with love she went.

Encouraged here, relieved pain there, brought hope;

Her tender words, an angel heaven sent.

Crimean wounded, lay in agony.

Death rate was nearly half. Then Britain's call;

She brought trained nurses, sanitary rules,

Supplies, devoted care; saved nearly all.

Returning home, health broken gave her life

To hospital reform, nurse colleges.

When India was torn with "mutiny"

Demanded health aid rural villages.

Heroic years for sick and suffering sealed

Her soul would ever inspiration yield.

*Hymn 567: "Thine Arm, O Lord, in Days of Old Was Strong to
    Heal and Save"*

*August 13*
*Bishop of Down Connor and Dromore, Strong Anglican Spirit in*
*Time of Political and Religious Turmoil. Died 1667*

# JEREMY TAYLOR

As loyal chaplain to King Charles the First
And to crushed army of the Royalists,
Harsh prison came with Cromwell's victory;
His rule fell on the land like iron fist.
Rejecting King's and Pope's authority,
He forced rough people's rule opposed to each.
Church windows, art and altars were destroyed.
Anglicans like Catholics they teach.
Then Taylor's forced retirement in Wales;
Wrote "Holy Living, Holy Dying," gifts.
In Liberty of Prophecy he pled
That faith and love in Christ heal human rifts.
When Monarchy restored, won Irish see.
Revived hurt churches, Prayer Book, pastored free.

*Hymn 518: "Christ Is Made the Sure Foundation"*

# JONATHAN MYRICK DANIELS

A "ministry of presence" was his goal

For civil rights and social justice' soul.

That long hot summer witnessed for Christ's love

King's caring Selma march strength from above.

When jailed for joining student picket line,

Refused his bail; not leave his friends behind.

Released, was shot on steps of grocery store;

Pushed girls in front to ground; no one gives more.

King said, "No incidents more beautiful

In all the annals of Church History.

The meaning of his life was so fulfilled,

Our grief gives way. Praise true nobility."

'Twas Mary's Son moved him to save the weak.

"He hath exalted humble and the meek."

*Hymn 593: "Lord, Make Us Servants of Your Peace"*

# ST. MARY THE VIRGIN

Her life and witness tells our faith in Christ
"Born of the Virgin," His humanity;
"Theotokus," "God-bearer," ancient Greeks;
Proclaims to world she bore Divinity
She represents the caring, holy Church
The vehicle of God to humankind
She was the ideal mother for her Son;
Returned from Temple last her love to find
She followed Him through all His ministry
Endured the pains that led Him to the Cross;
"John, Take her for your mother," Savior said
What last dear words of comfort in her loss
With Easter joy for souls disciples search;
What strength from Mary in the infant Church!

*Hymn 278: "Sing We of the Blessed Mother"*

# WILLIAM PORCHER DUBOSE

Virginia University, your sons
Fulfill proud founder Jefferson's best dreams.
This special son's creative Christian thought
Shared what the Holy Spirit's guidance means.
While chaplain in the War between the States
Last fortune, health, dear wife but not his call.
He built Sewanee's School, Theology –
Showed ancient faith is relevant for all.
Taught "Hebrew thoughts of priesthood, sacrifice,
Applied by Greeks and Gentiles to the cross,
Must live today; our thought, our speech, our lives."
Then Bible, creeds will save, not suffer loss.
"God placed before our eyes His own dear Son,
Believe that Christ is raised, our souls are won."

*Hymn 633: "Word of God Come Down on Earth"*

# BERNARD

Love warming faith in troubled Christian times;
His spirit touched men's hearts like saints of old.
Called last of Early Fathers moved the Church;
Revised Cistercian Order's life and mold.
He preached and lived a life of loving God:
"How kindly does He lead us in love's way —
How sweet is He to those who wait for Him!"[1]
His caring message lifted Europe's day.
He warned of heresies, lost Christian East.
He pled for kindness with our brother Jews.
He urged changed lives of prayer and charity.
New sixty abbeys now shared Christ's good news.
He begged the Church "that clothes her stones in gold,"
Leave not her sons still naked, "hungry, cold."

[1] *Bernard's,* On the Love of God

*Hymn 650: "O Jesus, Joy of Loving Hearts"*

# ST. BARTHOLOMEW

"Behold an Israelite in whom there is no guile."

Nathaniel puzzled, "How do you know me?"

"When you were under fig tree I saw you."

"Rabbi, you are the Son of God" for me. [1]

Three years of care, the Cross, but joy that dawn.

Last gift was breakfast shore by Galilee.

Heart moved with, "Go ye into all the world."

Armenia he sought for ministry.

Foundations laid for Christian Kingdom, first.

Then India, left Matthew's Gospel there. [2]

His martyrdom by shore of Caspean Sea;

His relics Rome and Canterbury, prayers. [3]

The purity that Jesus praised, "no guile,"

Calls us to rest in God each day awhile.

[1] *John 1:47 - 49*
[2] *Eusebius,* History of the Church. *pp.213-214*
[3] *D. H Farmer.* The Oxford Dictionary of
   Saints. *pp. 29-30*

*Hymn 280: "God of Saints to Whom the Number of the*
   *Starry Host Is Known"*

# LOUIS,
## KING OF FRANCE

As "knight in shining armor" led Crusades;

Like pious royal leaders of his day.

Yet his true gift to France was peace and law;

Curbed feudal warfare's sad misguided way;

Changed taxing system's sad inequities;

Taught every man should have his day in court;

Impartial, just with pure integrity;

Won Arab friends and English rare support.

As patron of wide learning and the arts,

Helped found great Paris University,

Cathedral Amiens, Bourges, and Chartres.

His patronage and spirit were their key.

Wrote, "Son, be kind," to poor and sick give hope.

"Praise God! Love Him." With His Love, Grace we cope.

*Hymn 279: "For Thy Dear Saints, O Lord"*

# THOMAS GALLAUDET & HENRY WINTER SYLE

The gift of hearing blesses us, what joy!

Inspired by his father's school for deaf,

Son dreamed their soul's potential to employ;

His church drew forth their creativity.

His service helped their relatives and friends;

Then afternoon reached deaf with worship's power;

Self confidence, life meaning were the end;

Day school, skill training, socials – life renewed!

New member, deaf was "God called" Henry Syle.

Lay reader, read for order, blest, ordained.

His caring love drew hearts of many, while

He founded All Souls' Church; gave hope, new lives.

Christ said, "He who has ears, then let him hear " [1]

For those who can't, two priests brought Jesus near.

*Thomas Gallaudet*

[1] *Revelation 2:7*

*Hymn 536: "God Has Spoken to His People"*

# AUGUSTINE OF HIPPO

Birth sprinkled with "Christ's salt" and signed with cross,
Since Paul no Call with greater promise heard;
Yet years of brilliant arrogance, vain search
For truth with intellect; wild pleasures lured.
Milan's wise, saintly Ambrose won his heart.
A garden cool, a storm of tears, child's voice,
"Take up and read." He seized God's word and saw:
"Come follow me"; then, "Put on Jesus Christ!"
Light calmed his soul, dear mother first to know.
Baptized, Rome solitude, then Hippo, home.
Priest, Bishop, Teacher; pastored ill and poor;
Fierce Vandals' siege left not his flock alone.
Prayer, Rule, Confessions free the Christian soul.
His God in History helps us see life whole.

*Hymn 671: "Amazing Grace!"*

# AIDAN

When gentle Aidan answered Oswald's call
To share his valiant kingdom's Christian stand,
Iona's love bloomed fresh in Lindisfarne,
Holy Island off Northumberland.
He built a school; he healed the sick and poor.
His sea retreat beyond protecting tides,
God's Sanctuary with a caring heart,
Sent forth bold pastors, teachers, spirit guides.
St. Bede recalls his love, humility,
His courage to rebuke the proud and cruel,
His tireless preaching tours at Oswald's side,
A life example for the Celtic Rule.
His final gift, young Cuthbert's Saintly goal,
Who saw bright Angels bearing Aidan's soul.

*Hymn 593: "Lord Make Me a Servant of Your Peace"*

*September 1*
*Deacon, Cheyenne Brave turned Servant of Christ*
*Died 1931*

# DAVID PENDLETON OAKERHATER

Tall warlike tribe, their lives with buffalo;

They chased the herds, their food and shelter lure.

Pushed westward, fought hard loss of hunting lands;

Wild chase, lives threatened, Custer massacre.

Imprisoned Florida, he found his Lord;

Released he was baptized, taking the name

Of David Pendleton. God called, ordained;

Returned and led his tribe, but not the same!

"Remember when I led you out to war.

Now I have learned about Christ Jesus, Lord

He is my Leader; all He tells is true.

Go with me now in war for peace," not sword.

Inspired warriors took up the Cross.

*Hymn 613: "Thy Kingdom Comes O God"*

156

# THE MARTYRS
# OF NEW GUINEA

Invasions brought much suffering and tears.

By choice, by force, protective policy,

Widespread remove of foreign clergy came.

Then Bishop Philip Strong gave moving plea,

"We must endeavor carry on our work.

Our God, our church at home expects of us.

The Universal Church expects of us.

The people whom we serve expect of us.

Could never hold our faces up again

If for our safety we forsook Him, fled."

They stayed; eight clergy, two lay workers killed.

Papua Christians carried on for dead.

They risked their lives, gave wounded, dying, care.

Young Church survived, with faith of martyrs there.

*Hymn 239: "Blessed Feasts of Blessed Martyrs"*

# PAUL JONES

"Behold how good and pleasant it is when
Brothers dwell in unity – the Lord
Commended blessing, life for evermore." [1]
Paul sought always the Bible healing word.
In Utah led the Church to love and grow;
Spoke movingly 'gainst violence, evil sign
Called World War I "unchristian"; anger rose;
The House of Bishops urged him to resign.
In farewell to his diocese he said,
"Where I serve church it matters not as long
As I make my life count in cause of Christ."
Expedience can not demean faith conscience wrong.
Until his death served ministry of peace.
So Gospel call to love might never cease.

*[1] Psalm 133*

*Hymn 598: "Lord Christ, When First Thou*
*Cam'st to Earth, Upon a Cross Thy Bound Thee"*

# CONSTANCE & HER COMPANIONS

In Memphis, Tennessee disaster struck;

Dread yellow fever plague left thousands dead.

Cathedral of St. Mary's, Children's Home

Were shelters where massed sick and dying fled.

Church staff and Sisters of St. Mary nursed

With tender love along each makeshift ward.

First sister stricken, Constance, gasped last words,

"Hosanna, Alleluia" saw her Lord?

Safe sisters on retreat came rushing home;

Ruth Theala, sister's chaplain, Schuyler, died;

Headmistress, Frances, most home children lost.

Charles Parsons, canon, final message cried,

"Lord Jesus Christ, receive my spirit here."

Such faith moves us; such witness, awesome, dear.

*Hymn 644: "How Sweet the Name of Jesus Sounds"*

# ALEXANDER CRUMMELL

He struggled with racism all his life.

New York refused his Holy Orders goal.

In Massachusetts finally made priest.

But Diocese denied convention role.

He sought Liberia for mission home;

Urged blacks to immigrate, build vibrant church

Warm energy, no longer there oppressed.

Support and politics killed noble search.

When southern bishops wanted separate

Black missionary district he opposed;

The union Black Episcopalians

Was born! The Church for all he first proposed.

Heroic life that Christians might be one;

His people's gifts share Christ with everyone.

*Hymn 529: "In Christ There Is No East or West, in Him No*
*South or North"*

# JOHN HENRY HOBART

Our quiet church slept waiting for its call.

New Nation's spirit gifts were yet to be.

God's people needed guidance from Above

To build a land of faith, love purity.

Young priest, ordained by founding Bishop White;

Taught Apostolic urgency for souls'

As bishop preached like Paul in every town;

Inspired clergy missionary roles;

Brought Christ to Indians, long dispossessed;

Established new prayer book society.

His tracts helped even British Anglicans;

His vision General Seminary's key.

Lord grant to us such missionary zest.

Our times need more of Thee before we rest.

*Hymn 657: "Love Divine, All Loves Excelling"*

# CYPRIAN

God called a proud aristocrat to Life,

To change from world's success, seek peace of soul.

He sold estates and gardens for the poor;

Baptized, explored belov'd church fathers' goal

Of saving lives for Christ's true kingdom Home.

When asked to lead now persecuted flock,

Consoled the martyred, pastored those who lapsed,

Made apostolic faith their saving rock.

When plague filled streets with terror, dying, dead,

He organized wide loving healing care.

Yet Church was blamed for angered Roman gods;

All clergy ordered executed there.

The weeping throngs stood by him to the end;

Last words, "Thanks be to God." What faith to send!

*Hymn 524: "I Love Thy Kingdom Lord, the House of Thine Abode"*

# HOLY CROSS DAY

Helena found It on the holy hill
Where Christ, God's only Son, was crucified.
Her son, blest Constantine, great emperor,
Asked her to save the place Christ rose and died.
She supervised two shrines to tell the world
Of Grace that came Christ's resurrection day:
Basilica for liturgy of "word"
The Resurrection Altar where tomb lay.
Between these shrines where faithful had to pass
From Word to Sacrament was Calvary:
Its top expense moved hearts to meditate;
"Here loving Lord once died and rose for me."
God bless dear faithful friends from long ago
Who spent your lives our souls deep faith might know!

*Hymn 441: "In the Cross of Christ I Glory"*

# NINIAN

Our blessed Lord seeks always for lost sheep.

Fierce Scottish clans long sought for peace and light.

God called a chieften's son in that torn land,

A Christian lad to help them love, not fight.

He found at Rome great teachers of the faith

Was consecrated Bishop, preach for souls;

Spent months at Tours; became St. Martin's friend;

Monastic-mission way now formed his goals.

He built St. Martin's Church in Galloway

Called "White House" for its rare white walls of stone.

His Abbey's teaching, healing care for all

Gave Scottish Picts new hope; now Christ their own;

Like Alban's fearless Roman Britain stand

And David's Wales and Patrick's Ireland.

*Hymn 539: "O Zion Haste Thy Mission High Fulfilling"*

# HILDEGARD

Church raised by Jutta, anchoress of faith,
In cottage near a Benedictine Home.
Drawn by their life of silence and of prayer
More women joined them seeking peace their own.
From childhood, visions thrilled her loving soul;
Inspired writings, drawings moved faith hopes.
Church blessed her work. Her counsel sought
By kings and queens, archbishops, even popes.
Her worship music was described as "Chant –
Surpassing sweet the melody – unheard."
Her "Play of Virtues" each one sang their part,
But devil was condemned to sing no word!
She practiced medicine, sought women's needs.
Her caring spirit planted healing seeds.

*Hymn 376: "Joyful, Joyful, We Adore Thee"*

# EDWARD BOUVERIE PUSEY

The Church in England drifted; faith confused.

Victorians of upper class were dilettante;

They dabbled lightly in their church affairs.

Renowned John Newman sought Rome's holy tent.

Tracts for the Times appeared to save such loss.

Here Pusey helped affirm faith gifts divine,

Christ's saving presence in the Eucharist.

Confession private cleanses sins, yours, mine.

His family fortune gave to lowest poor;

Safe homes for orphans, free trade schools to save;

St John's Evangelist Society;

New Sisterhoods served cradle to the grave.

"The poor of Christ are Church's special treasure."[2]

In serving them we have Him without measure.

[1] Saints Galore, *David Veal.*
[2] *From a Christmas Sermon by Edward Pusey*
   *entitled "God with Us"*

*Hymn 304: "I Come With Joy to Meet My Lord"*

# THEODORE OF TARSUS

From St. Paul's native city came strong help

For plague sick, strife torn, weakened English church.

They needed Bishop who would make all one;

To reconcile and heal began his search.

Traditions of the Celts and Catholics

Respected; came together in his care.

He built great school to train and educate;

Christ's version of one family grew there [1]

His kindness drew – like Bishop Chad who said,

"I never thought myself worthy of it."

Archbishop made him Bishop, Mercia!

With love the scattered Christians now were knit

Into a caring whole with diocese;

More pastors moved; brought tense, heard souls release.

[1] *John 17: 20-23*
[2] *Bede,* A History of the English Church
   and People; *Bk. 4, Chap. 2-3*

*Hymn 643: "My God, How Wonderful Thou Art"*

# JOHN COLERIDGE PATTESON

Young Oxford graduate, John, heard his call:
New Zealand's Bishop, "Help us spread the light."
On Norfolk island he built school for boys,
Youth leaders trained, know Christ and share your sight.
For twenty years led hospitals and schools;
Church teaching centers, sacraments, healed fears.
He ministered to British settlers there;
Confirmed the Pitcairn Island mutineers.
He fought to stop "blackbirding" seizing slaves'
Brought ship, The Southern Cross, to Nakapu;
Ashore to comfort grieving homes, was killed;
Some mistook friend who cared, companions too.
"You can't remake your hearts; He must do it —
You must be born again." John died for this.

*Hymn 537: "Christ for the World We Sing"*

# ST. MATTHEW

He watched in isolation as the crowd
So grimly entered his tax office door;
Respectful words, yet eyes that flickered scorn;
Prestige and wealth were his, but friends no more.
Then 'cross the room he saw one gentle face;
The Lord came close and shared how life could be.
Position, things, all faded in that Light.
The "Way" alone remained and "Follow me?"
What gems his Gospel saved of Jesus then!
The Tax Collectors' Feast of humble men,
The Wise Men, Star, the Sermon on the Mount,
Child raised, blessed "Inasmuch," Lost Sheep that count,
His Voice across the waves, "Fear not, 'tis I,"
His call, "Give all and follow me" on high.

*Hymn 560: " Remember Your Servants, Lord,"*

# SERGIUS

Brave Christians agonized 'neath Tartars' yoke;

Fierce pagans drove his family from home.

They farmed near Moscow where he felt his call

To seek as forest hermit Christ his own.

His brother, Stephen, first; then pilgrims found

Same forest wild; saw prayer and Scripture start

Love care for others, filling souls with joy.

A monastery grew, touched Russia's heart.

Peace keeper midst the quarreling princes there;

Encouraged stand 'gainst Tartar overlords,

"A simple, humble, grave and gentle saint,"

Yet patriot, helped sheath rough nations' swords.

Saw Virgin's vision with the liturgy;

His Light – changed features sometimes one could see.

*Hymn 73: "The King Shall Come When Morning Dawns"*

*September 26*
*Bishop of Winchester, Scholar, Preacher, Pastor of 17th Century*
*England. Died 1626*

# LANCELOT ANDREWES

"Oh thou who very early while the sun

Was yet arising didst rise from the dead,

Rise us up daily unto newness life;

Suggest repentance ways" our souls are fed. [1]

From such deep prayer he preached God's "blessed word,"

"The means to raise our souls to joy today,

The pledge to raise our bodies evermore;

He authored both. His righteousness our way." [2]

Court sermons moved Elizabeth and James;

King's Bible authorized, he helped translate;

Defended English church's heritage;

Care – pastored all; God's mercies Heaven's gate.

With Catholics and Puritans shared love;

So lived the faith and peace that leads above.

[1] *Private Devotions, "The Dial"*
[2] *Sermons, "Of the Resurrection," Easter 1620*

*Hymn 525: "The Church's One Foundation*
*Is Jesus Christ Her Lord"*

# ST. MICHAEL & ALL ANGELS

Their wings are all around us like God's love.

The Lord has plans for us we may not see;

His glory dreams for us we may not dream;

But ask His will, He'll give glad ministry.

His caring may not bring relief from pain;

Yet taking Him to others and our own

Brings healings, peace, and miracles of joy;

In asking for our cross we find our home.

St. Michael is the Captain of them all,

Protector seeking souls and searching hearts.

Feel for his spirit help when testing comes;

He brings Christ's power to help our new life starts.

So let us live that other lives may sing.

Each difference made may brush an angel's wing.

*Hymn 282: "Christ the Fair Glory of the Holy Angels"*

# JEROME

A restless, prideful youth with passions wild,
A brilliant mind, trained classically in Rome,
Long Sunday walks in Christian catacombs–
Heart touched, baptized, a path to lead him Home.
In Gaul was drawn toward deep ascetic life.
From Antioch sought peace in hermit cave.
His massive, Godly learning recognized,
Gave rest of life the word of God to save.
Dear Bethlehem became his soul's workshop.
From Greek and Hebrew scriptures, faith set free;
Released with love, Good News would never stop.
Translated Latin Bible sure to spread.
Reviewing Jeremiah when he died –
An honored saint at last, self-crucified.

*Hymn 637: "O Christ, the Word Incarnate,*
    *O Wisdom from on High"*

# REMIGIVS

"Now worship what you burned!" King Clovis heard;

Three thousand Franks were baptized that great day.

"Then burn what you have worshipped," Bishop charged;

As humbly to their Christ they knelt to pray.

He gave his life to reach the pagan Franks

With love of God and Christian peaceful way.

They brought the Holy Faith to Germany;

They freed the church of Gaul from Roman sway.

Proud Rheims Cathedral, What magnificence!

Rose window still our pilgrim steps enthrall.

St. Augustine renewed the English heart.

Encouraged by support from Christian Gaul.

Dear Remi, thank you for your caring soul,

Your wisdom, teaching, faith helps make us whole.

*Hymn 518: "Christ Is Made the Sure Foundation"*

# FRANCIS OF ASSISI

A pleasure-loving youth rode off to war
To find his purpose, manhood, nobler goal.
Soon, horror sickened, he returned disgraced
To seek another path for lonely soul.
St. Damian long heard his troubled prayers;
"Rebuild my Church," God's answer seemed to say;
Maturing thought saw "Church" meant suffering lives;
His "Lady Poverty" inspired the way.
He nursed the lepers, healed the hurt and sad.
Rome's Holy Father blessed his joyous band.
Stigmata crowned devotion to his Lord.
His Rule of loving service blessed the land.
Those tireless caring footsteps echo still;
They call to love, Christ's Kingdom to fulfill.

*Hymn 400: "All Creatures of Our God and King"*

# WILLIAM TYNDALE

He dreamed a Bible every child could read.

When Oxford student Scriptures touched his heart.

When priested taught God's Word to nurture souls.

But Latin was for most a scholar's art.

Commenced an English Bible for all men.

His labors Church and crown sought to suppress.

He fled to continent to save his life.

Blind fear of change pursued, forced cruel stress.

Harassed and hounded from each refuge place,

Translates New Testament, first part of Old,

Betrayed by friend, condemned for heresy,

Yet his great phrases lived, true spirit gold.

At stake as strangled, burned he bravely cries

"Last words," "Lord, open King of England's eyes."

*Hymn 631: "Book of Books, Our Peoples' Strength"*

# ROBERT GROSSETESTE

He loved all people. Lincoln's Bishop gave
Blest pastoral example, souls to save.
He visited each deanery with care,
Preached, taught, removed the lazy clergy there.
To lead just worship time is not enough;
True priests should comfort all whose lives are rough;
The hungry feed, the sinful guide to peace,
The underpaid, the overworked release.
He fought Rome's priests made rector absentees
To get his vacant church's salaries!
"Hands to the jaws of death sad thousands' souls."
Neglect destroys faith, Christians' promised goals.
Said "I am obligated visit sheep";
"Scripture prescribes" their lives and hearts to keep.

*Hymn 513: "Like the Murmur of the Dove's Song"*

# PHILIP, DEACON & EVANGELIST

One of those seven noble holy men

Who helped Apostles, poor, sick, old-love care.

Then Spirit led him to Samaria;

He preached the Gospel, brought faith, healing there.

He won their hearts, baptized them in the Lord.

Then Angel spoke, "Go down the Gaza road."

He met an Ethiopian, confused,

Isaiah's words, Messiah's coming told.

He shared Lord Jesus' life and Easter joy.

Baptized the traveler, now Savior's own

Again the Spirit sent him on to preach

In all the towns 'til Caesarea home.

Four daughters prophesied, moved hearts of all.

One more blessed time – last trip he hosted Paul!

*Hymn 528: "Lord, You Give the Great Commission"*

# EDWARD THE CONFESSOR

His subjects said, "He lived an angel's life."
Last Saxon King before the Norman strife,
He served the lowly poor with loving care;
His gift of healing never failed to share.
A friend at Mass, beside him, saw the Lord;
When told, rapt Edward said, "I too adored."
His Abbey, Peter's house of timeless prayer;
What heroes of the faith are treasured there!
In name of John a pilgrim begged the King;
To honor that dear Saint he gave his ring.
Years later it was sent from 'cross the sea
With old man's word, "I'm John; you'll be with me."
Epiphany's glad Eve, beside his Queen,
He met his Lord with praise, and faith serene.

*Hymn 614: "Christ Is the King"*

# SAMUEL ISAAC JOSEPH SCHERESCHEWSKY

Inclined at first to seek the Rabbinate,

Found Christ in scripture, prayers with German friends.

Sought ministry with Presbyterians;

Episcopal church claimed his life's great ends.

When Bishop Boone implored more China help

He volunteered, learned Chinese on the sea;

First wrote the Bible into Mandarin;

Then founded St. John's University.

When paralyzed, resigned yet struggled on;

In Wenli dialect whole Bible gave;

Two thousand pages with his crippled hand;

One finger tapped the Gospel love to save.

Wise Chinese give their scholars great respect,

Find faith in words and lives their hearts expect.

*Hymn 529: "In Christ There Is No East or West"*

# TERESA OF AVILA

"If Jesus dwells in one of us as friend

And noble leader, all thing we endure —

For Christ helps strengthens us; He is true friend.

Blessed is the one who loves him, keeps him near.

Inspired by the letters of Jerome,

In youthful illness found her inner light.

Sweet charm, high spirits, prudence, charity

Endeared her in her convent, Carmelite.

The lives of Magdalene and Augustine

Led soul conversion, visions, deeper prayer.

She founded sixteen convents, primitive,

Hard work and service, worship, loving care.

Heirs of the Renaissance learned faith to cope.

Her writings, lived in Grace, still blossom hope.

*Hymn 302: "Father, We Thank Thee"*

# HUGH LATIMER & NICHOLAS RIDLEY

Two heroes died in flames for conscience sake.
What horrors had they done to justify?
Attracted to reforms on continent,
Supporting his Archbishop's path to die
For teaching worship, faith free English way;
Though Nicholas acquitted heresy,
When London's Bishop, burned for his belief.
Friend Latimer resigned Worcester's See
Protesting King's reactionary drive
Against the Reformation's progress goals.
He preached for moral values, caring lives
That Christians by example win new souls.
Last words to Ridley, "Play the man! We light
By grace a fire never gone from sight."

*Hymn 237: "Let Us Now Our Voices Raise"*

# THOMAS CRANMER

It was a time that tried the souls of men;

The English Church reforming for new start;

Like Alban, Patrick, David, Ninian

Renewed the faith for many seeking heart.

"Rome's Bishop has no more authority

Than any foreign bishop here," he said;

Composed first English Prayer Book all could read;

Fresh liturgy, deep bible study led.

When Mary Tudor gained the English throne

She tried to force her people back to Rome.

Imprisoned Cranmer, facing torture, death,

Denied the faith that truly was his own.

When tied to stake recanted his denial;

Thrust hand that signed it first into the fire.

*Hymn 680: "O God Our Help in Ages Past"*

# IGNATIUS OF ANTIOCH

Devout old man being led to Rome in chains,

Adoring Christ, can't worship Trajan's name.

To keep true faith would mean a martyr's death,

Yet God in Jesus he must ever claim.

Along the way still feeds each faithful flock;

Their loving prayers keep strong his fearless soul.

His grateful letters share the Cause Divine:

One Christian family, the Shepherd's goal.

They also tell a bishop's gracious love;

His own bereaved, dear church now waits alone.

He goes to die with Christ, the Perfect Man,

And rise with Him to be forever home.

"I am God's wheat, when ground by teeth of beast;

I'll be true bread of Christ," to share the feast.

*Hymn 517: "How Lovely Is Thy Dwelling Place"*

# ST. LUKE

Belov'd Physician, first at Troas heard
Apostle preach the liberating Word.
He grasped the truth of healing through the soul,
Committed rest of life to this pure goal.
The Lord's compassion filled his thoughtful mind:
In Good Samaritan, what care we find!
In Prodigal, forgiveness, love and peace;
Zachaeus, how confession brings release.
What faith he learned from Mary's memories,
Our dear Lord's birth, the angel melodies!
What courage, watching Paul trust God each day
Through jail to death beside the Appian Way.
Theophilus, good patron, you may know
The blessings, still, that from your wisdom flow.

*Hymn 449: "O Love, How Deep, How Broad, How High"*

# HENRY MARTYN

Heart moved by Cambridge Chaplain, Simeon,

He shared Christ's love through India the East:

Calcutta's churches, Patna, campus schools;

He sought God's people, mightiest and least.

His Hindu Prayer Book and New Testament

Brought faith, soul peace throughout that ancient land.

In Shirmas, Persia, was first English priest;

Christ's written Gospel brought them by his hand.

He longed to reach Arabia for God;

Exhausted came to Turkey dying in prayer.

Last days with Christians from Armenia

Who buried him with Bishop's honor there.

"Go into all the world," His Master said,

From Henry's precious years, now millions fed.

*Hymn 531: "O Spirit of the Living God"*

# ST. JAMES
# OF JERUSALEM

Concerned when Jesus left to call the Twelve,

With family sent plea through crowd, "Come home!"

Alarmed as fateful opposition grew;

Saw mother stand by Cross, her Son, her own.

Then Brother's love, before Ascension Day,

Appeared to him. He gave his life in trust.

When Stephen stoned, Apostles spread the word;

Elected James 1st Bishop, called the "Just."

When Paul brought news of Gentile's turn to God,

James welcomed all who saving Gospel heard.

He led his flock with purity and prayer.

He wrote to all, "Be doers of the Word."

Though told to cease, preached Christ with every breath

Was hurled from Temple; witnessed by his death.

*Hymn 576: "Here in Christ We Gather"*

# ALFRED THE GREAT

Alone of British Rulers called, "The Great";
His courage, caring virtues saved his land.
Blessed by Pope Leo Fourth at age of four,
'Gainst Viking raiders made heroic stand;
'Til Danish Captain, Gunthrum, stopped at last;
Then won to baptism, Christ's peaceful Way;
Made Southern, even Midlands Regions safe
For culture, learning, faith to win the day.
The Classics, Augustine, Pope Gregory, wise Bede
Had translated to help his clergy teach.
His justice, fairness, founded English Law.
His palace school taught nobler life to reach.
He sought for all God-trust he held most dear –
"That endless life where all shall be made clear."

*Hymn 585: "Morning Glory, Starlit Sky"*

# ST. SIMON & ST. JUDE

They saw their risen Lord on Easter Day.

They set out with the rest new souls to search.

Simon called the zealot drew men's hearts.

Jude wrote, "Contend for faith" saints saved for Church.

Tradition says each traveled far for Christ;

Bold Simon showed old Egypt Christian care;

Jude taught where Tigris and Euphrates roll;

They joined to preach in Persia, martyred there.

Their relics moved in love St. Peter's Rome.

Art shows Simon's fish; Jude's club, life's cost.

Jude's help and guidance often been implored.

By those with causes desperate or lost.

Last words, "To only God our Savior be

Glory, power and authority."

*Jude 1:3 and 25*

*Hymn 232: "Praise Lord for Your Apostles"*

# JAMES HANNINGTON

"Dark Continent" called to his caring heart.

He volunteered to share Christ's healing peace.

Victoria, Nyanza felt his love

'Til illness drove him home to find release.

Came back as Bishop, seeking souls for God,

To Lake Victoria a mission chain.

Uganda's new King, Mwanga, feared, believed

A stranger from the east would end his reign;

Sent warriors to stop him at the Nile.

James, speared and dying, cried, "Go tell your king,

I die for all the people of our land;

My blood has bought the way." What Offering!

One hundred years, again Christ's martyrs save;

"Luwum, Archbishop, Life blooms from your grave."

*Hymn 690: "Guide Me, Oh Thou Great Jehovah"*

# SEASONS AND HOLY DAYS

# ADVENT

Isaiah told the coming of God's reign
The sacred story of God's people tells
Lord's ancient plan Messiah now to be
A promise of sweet distant Christmas bells
"Repent! Prepare your hearts," the Baptist cried;
Then Jesus humbly sought baptism, John
"This is my beloved Son, hear Him,"
Then Christ called Twelve, taught them to carry on
With words and acts of selfless love He gave
Won hearts and souls by shores blue Galilee
He tried Jerusalem to win hard unbelief;
In Second Coming joy then all shall see
Oh cleanse our hearts, dear Lord, bring hope again
Our hope depends on Child of Bethlehem.

*Hymn 66: "Come Thou Long Expected Jesus"*

# CHRISTMAS

Glad songs of healing, hope and holy joy.
The angels, shepherds heard and found the Boy
Three Wise men followed ever bright'ning star;
Their visions led where worlds' true glories are.
Ambassadors of faith all knelt in awe;
Returned and shared the love of God they saw.
When holy Jesus smiled with Mary's care
Protecting Joseph's arms held both so fair.
Oh joy for all of God's great Christmas Day!
Oh joy when heaven on earth her warm heart lay.
Oh baby Jesus, through the world you gave
New hope for love to ever heal and save.
May Christ our Christmas gift bring lasting glory
Fill the world with hope; begin new story.

*Hymn 111: "Silent Night Holy Night"*

# EPIPHANY

Majestic kings arrive the stable door.

They kneel among the sheep on stable floor.

God gave them insight, worship of the child;

Returned to tell the world their journey wild.

For faith in simple things oft wins the day,

Like reaching for the stars drives sins away.

Then came his Holy Baptism so dear.

God's word from heaven blessed his Son, no fear.

First miracle at Cana's wedding feast;

Changed water into wine and faith increased

So glad three ways the Son was shown to be

The power of hope and love for all to see.

O join this host and help to conquer world.

No more shall sin and doubt keep banners furled.

*Hymn 124: "What Star Is This?"*

# LENT

Lent is a "love song" * always meant to be;
Between two lovers, God humanity;
For God gave everything — beloved man
So both would live in loving harmony.
Long centuries of anger, cruelty
Made Lent and all that's good a mockery.
'Til sons of God stretched out their arms in hope
Along hard narrow way they learned to cope.
And see! The Way is brave, hope victory
The cross is empty land so beautiful.
God breathed new life along the restless sea
In hearts "prayer ready" to be "spirit full."
So Lent's a "love song" * never, never ends;
It's God's life breath within dear sons and friends.

* The Rev. Judith Heffron, title to essay.

Hymn 143: "The Glory of These Forty Days"

# PALM SUNDAY

Almighty God, we praise you for your gifts
Of love by which you have redeemed our lives;
Through your Son, Jesus Christ, our Savior, Lord.
This day, Jerusalem, the Holy City, cries,
"Blest is He who comes in the name of Lord."
"Blest is His coming Kingdom, David's Son."
"Hosanna in the highest!" sang their joy.
Psalms blest triumphant way, yet Cross begun.
He cleansed the temple, drove out thieving crowd;
Isaiah wrote, "My house, a house of prayer."
The blind and lame, He healed them everyone.
"From lips of children" glad praise filled the air.
What hope and faith for hearts who worshipped there!
The King of Kings, our Christ, God's love and care.

*Hymn 154: "All Glory, Laud and Honor"*

# MAUNDY THURSDAY

He said to Peter, John, "Go now, prepare
Where with disciples I may eat last meal"
The Passover, dear Feast, glad memory
When God led Israel to freedom real
Hushed awe around the rev'rent table there
"This broken bread my body" for your soul
"This cup my blood" poured out for you in love
"Do this remembering me," look for your goal
When I am gone the Holy Spirit comes;
He will fulfill your joy still yet to see.
They went once more Gethsemane to pray
He knelt alone, "Lord, take this cup from me."
In deeper prayer, "Not my will, thine be done"
He blessed them all; His Kingdom had begun!"

*Hymn 315: "Thou, Who at Thy First Eucharist Didst Pray"*

# GOOD FRIDAY, THE TRIAL

Why good they say, yet here God's greatest gift?

His own dear Son to cancel all our sins.

Yet through that grief and struggle there

Our hope and trusting humble faith still wins.

When Pilot heard the Son of God, his name

He sought to follow dear wife's true advice.

"Have none to do with this true righteous man"

But coward Pilot couldn't be that nice.

So Jesus dragged in like a criminal;

Became excuse to quiet angry mob.

Perhaps as Son of God was sent to die

One might have heard bewildered Pilot sob.

"If you are Son of God then save us too."

"Forgive them for they know not what they do."

*Hymn 474: "When I Survey the Wondrous Cross"*

# GOOD FRIDAY, THE CRUCIFIXION

They taunted God's true blessed only Son.
They tried to break his faith and body too.
"Son, Dear Son, behold your Mother true."
"Mother, Dear Mother, to John be mother too."
He took her to his home by western sea
Now Mary's house in Ephesus brings hope
To countless pilgrims seeking faith to cope
Her life of pain and hope faith's mystery
"Into thy hands commend my spirit" last
Then soldiers came limp body ground they cast
But holy women took him, borrowed tomb
Wait for Easter day and Love to bloom.
Holy Saturday was lonely, cold;
Easter Sunday bright with spirit gold.

*Hymn 172: "Were You There When they Crucified My Lord?"*

# HOLY SATURDAY

The day dawned bitter cold and grim.
The apostles hiding fearful without Him.
The whole world, lost with breathing seemed to stop
The energy of all things seemed to drop
Yet Faith still nursed their saddened hearts of doom.
His words of promise to come back pierced gloom.
Each sought some comfort in his special way
For would not next dawn be the special day?
Earth rested all that night so sad and dim.
For hope to win or weakness, special sin.
Birds started chirping as the dawn appeared;
Made brave by terror thoughts no longer feared.
Apostles woke to find their better day.
The women took the spices on their way.

*Hymn 173: "O Sorrow Deep!"*

# EASTER DAY

Dear Easter day, glad Easter day; life new!
No fear of death, our Christ gave all for you.
Follow Him, no matter where he leads.
We trust his guidance, plant His love's best seeds.
How many hearts will brighten in the glow
Of love from Him whom makes our spirits grow?
Spring flowers raise their blossoms in the sun
As if to say in spirit, all are one.
Dear Mary Magdalene runs from the tomb
Apostles greet Him in their hiding room
Disciples meet him hopeful mystery.
He breaks the supper bread their eyes now see!
Great earth awakens to a new found hope
Of strength to conquer sin and faith to cope.

*Hymn 207: "Jesus Christ Is Risen Today"*

# ASCENSION

The day of earthly parting had to be.
Sweet years of closeness here, but now were done.
They had to let him go to keep him still
One poignant moment then gone like the Sun.
He rose with majesty in bright blue sky;
Their hopes and dreams of all the years fulfilled.
But ere his sight was gone three holy men
Said, "Men of Galilee why gaze thee so?
He promised you all hope a man could have
He will return just as you saw him go;
Cling to his promises each hard long day;
A better life will be yours now to know.
Dear Christ, now in his home above,
Will win his world at last to sharing love."

*Hymn 214: "Hail the Day That Sees Him Rise"*

# PENTECOST

Apostles needed help to face the world.
Around their mission myriad questions swirled;
Now all the earth must fully understand
Their call could transform every bit of land.
From serving cruelty and lust for gain
To force for righteousness like healing rain.
God's will is world of plenitude for all.
For spirit life true angel food we call.
Pray Holy Spirit, fill us with insight
To make each land, each home a shining light.
Give us the power to heal each selfish wound
Grant us the courage to not faint or swoon.
Come Holy Spirit, we give our hearts to thee;
God bless us, all thy servant helpers be.

*Hymn 510: "Come Holy Spirit"*

# THANKSGIVING

From hopeful dreams to greater godly glory
We spread new freedom far as Pacific West
We welcomed Europe's tired huddled masses,
Their talents newly shared were truly blessed.
With Christian grace we sought humility
That others like us truly might be free
Yet human frailty crept in to hold us back
Our pains today come from so much we lack
Perceived as braggarts need to share our fortune
Both spirit given and material resource
In struggling world shared love is healing force
Come now Lord Jesus let us live thy way
For actions our live words bring hope today
Use us just as thou will each sharing day.

*Hymn 443: "We Gather Together to Ask the*
*Lord's Blessing"*

# SPECIAL MOMENTS WITH SPECIAL SAINTS

*St. Boniface, Archbishop of Mainz*

I was sad as I left St. Boniface's beautiful Cathedral in September of 1967. I had found no pictures, or a window about him. It was time to take the tram back to Frankfurt to rejoin my family. I tried to hail a taxi, but they just sped by me. Watching others, I saw you had to step out in the street to hail one. When I finally reached the station and raced to my train track, it was already moving out!

When a second train pulled in I climbed aboard and looked for a seat; all were taken and commuters were standing in the aisles. Way down one car there appeared to be a vacant seat. I reached and claimed it and then understood why it was open. It was next to a Roman Catholic priest! Being unimpressed by someone in my profession we fell into easy conversation. He was on furlough from his post in Japan after many years. I shared my failed search for memories of St. Boniface. I knew he had been buried at Fulda where his sister had been head of a convent but we were leaving for America in the morning. I would never get to his grave and shrine in Fulda. I would go home with not even a picture of it.

He reached into his pocket and pulled out a pamphlet all about Fulda and St. Boniface's shrine. "Is this what you wanted, my son?" as he handed it to me! I was overcome with joy and gratitude. I was not supposed to be on this train! The only seat was beside him. He was home from Japan for the first time in years. He had just been to Fulda and St. Boniface's tomb.

Thank you; Lord. You want me to pursue my dream of sharing the faith and heritage of the saints. Thank you, Lord, you helped me find St. Boniface.

## Epilogue

*Thomas á Kempis, author of* The Imitation of Christ

It was late Saturday in 1967 when we drove into Zwolle, Holland. I wanted to find some memories of blessed Thomas, one of our Episcopal saints. We stopped at the library, but a street carnival made it impossible to park. We drove to the Cathedral. My children, son-in-law and my wife hinted that I had picked a busy time to find a picture of a memorial window. They wanted to get on to our reservations in Utrecht and dinner.

Inside the Cathedral were many penitents waiting to make their confessions before Sunday Mass. I looked mainly at the walls and windows — nothing of Thomas to be seen — and sadly entered the doorway to leave. I saw a well dressed man just entering. Some strange impulse made me say to him, "Sir, do you know anything about Thomas á Kempis?" He responded, "Yes, I've made a study of him." I told him of my search for pictures and memories to go with a dreamed of book of sonnets about the saints. He said, "Come to my home tonight. I have everything you want."

I struggled with my conscience. I could pressure the family. What a great chance, but then no, this was their trip too. They had patiently taken me to many saints' shrines already. I told Mr. Erftemeiner "I can't today, but maybe I can write to you?" We exchanged addresses.

Back at the mini-bus the family was patiently waiting. As we started for Utrecht again, it started to rain, but the children begin to sing. My heart felt warm. They were happy. "Thank you, Lord, for the right decision and for the miraculous contact at the Cathedral doors." Weeks later, colored slides arrived with remembrances of Thomas such as Thomas á Kempis High School! In 1980, Nellie and I visited Dr. Erftemeiner on our retirement trip. He met us at the train and hosted us at his home the night of his birthday party. The next day he drove us all around Zwolle and to the special memorial cross for Thomas á Kempis in the ruins of the old Agnetenberg monastery where Thomas had written his world-famous, life-changing book for so many in his day and still ours. People came to him for counseling from all over Europe. "Thanks, Lord, again, for leading us to Thomas."

## St. Augustine of Hippo

At St. Ambrose's Cathedral in Milan in 1967, the "Ambrosia" as it is called, I inquired about the final resting place of the remains of St. Augustine of Hippo of North Africa. The priest couldn't speak English but he just said, "Pavia," a nearby Italian city.

Although he gave me no specific directions, we knew we had to explore Pavia. At the Cathedral we found nothing, but a priest pointed down a long street and said simply, "Augustine." We started out on foot. Soon we came to St. Mary's Church of the Asumption. We crossed the square and came to a church dedicated to "Pietro de Oro," St. Peter of the Gold – so named by Dante because of the gold painted ceiling. We entered quietly and walked down the center aisle toward the altar.

We stopped at a large ornate tomb just in front of the altar. This was it! Here lay the remains of the greatest theologian for Christ in the early church. We sank to our knees in prayer. We had found the shrine of the author of the monumental City of God and his Confessions. Our search for his shrine, his place of everlasting veneration was complete! Thank you, Lord.

## St. Irenaeus of Lyon

We were told to seek guidance for our search at the Basilique de Fourviere (the old church) on the hill. Here the secretary of the enormous sacristy drove us to the church of St. Irenee and St. Just. We passed on the basilica grounds the statue of St. Pothinus, martyred Bishop of Lyon in 178 AD! Father Clement, the pastor, met us at the church and arranged for a young French/English teacher to meet us at 4 p.m. after his class. René Arnaud showed us the crypt under the church which held the tomb of St. Irenaeus and other martyrs and the "well of the martyrs" where Blandina and the others were thrown. It was a holy place! We could sense how the church of St. Irenaeus and St. Just was hallowed by the heroes and heroines of the faith who had given their lives for our Christ in the second century!

What is their influence today? René Arnaud told us of the ongoing vibrant life of this historic parish. Once a year they have an all-day parish meeting to evaluate the past year and plan the next year's work, including education for adults in groups discussions with trained leaders, groups for retirees, for couples preparing for marriage, a group for planning music and liturgy. A parish bi-monthly paper gives both coming events and also ideas from the study and discussion groups. René leads their baptism preparation classes for families and children.

I went to the communion rail in the crypt for a moment to pray. What a miracle that we should find kind M. Serveux who would go out of his way to take us, in our limited time, to the one place essential for our quest; and then that the clergy there should, on short notice, arrange for us to meet the dear young English teacher who is himself so spiritually involved in the parish. He gave us a feeling of the living influence of the "Martyrs of Lyon" today.
I prayed:

> *"Dear God, please help us to tell these stories so that the timeless spirit of the saints may bring us closer to Christ and one another — all over the world today — in this great hour of the world's needs."*

As we were leaving, we met the sister on the staff and were given copies of both the crypt guide and the bi-monthly parish paper, "Letters to the Christians." Father Clement came to us at the last and smilingly accepted our *"Merci beaucoup!"* René Arnaud sends in the weekly parish programs each year.

## St. Patrick of Ireland

We spent ten wonderful days in this beautiful country, guests of the

Rev. and now Bishop Mayes, in Cork. We visited several St. Patrick places, including the rock where he baptized the King.

It was not recommended to go to dangerous northern Ireland, but Father Mayes arranged for a friend, the Rev. Charles Combs, to meet our train at Portadown and drive us to Armagh, where Patrick built his first church, now site of the present great Cathedral.

We met Canon Love who had us for tea and sherry after supper. Canon Love's name seemed so positive in that strife torn area, just what was needed most! The next day we took a bus to Belfast and explored the Cathedral at Downpatrick where Patrick is buried. The big stone rock over his resting place has big letters carved with – PATRICK. The special church windows tell some of his story.

Then we took a bus to the village of Saul and the little church built there in 1933, to remember his landing there on his return to Ireland as a Bishop in 432. This church marks the 1,500 years that the faith has bloomed in Ireland after his return. The little church breathed a timeless spirit when we entered. Then we sat on the garden wall and enjoyed the first warm sunshine in days.

Birds, butterflies and bees were all around us in this special place of memory, truly a sanctuary for the soul we felt, in a land so torn by anger and strife.

We prayed that the peace of the soul that is worth everything, will spread from truly holy places like treasured Saul.

## St. Columba, Iona, Scotland

I first sought him alone in 1967. From Oban a train took me across the island of Mull to the Iona ferry. From the beginning this green, hilly, white sheep dotted little island, felt special.

At the inn the desk lady greeted me, "We were expecting you, Rev. Saville. Welcome." Her words were not surprising, since I had made reservations ahead in London; but then a maid appeared at the end of the long room and called out, "I'll show you to your room, Rev. Saville." What a friendly, prepared-for welcome!

That evening I went to the service at St. Michael's Chapel at the old Abbey. It was a communion service. They have a heart-warming custom of two people sharing one piece of consecrated bread in the courtyard afterwards. I shared with a young college student there on a special trip. As we talked of our families and reasons for being there, I felt a warmth as though we were not far from the first Christ-consecrated Holy Table.

I returned to Iona in 1980, with my wife, Nellie Anne, and my son, John, and daughter-in-law, Kathleen. The same caring and sanctuary feeling was there. The Abbey has a social work for poor and needy in Glasgow. We explored the "White Strand of the Monks," where Norsemen in longboats had landed and made martyrs of faithful monks. We walked past the "Hill of the Angels" to the southern tip of the island at "St. Columba's Bay." He and fellow monks landed and could stay because it fulfilled his penance of not seeing his beloved Ireland again until he had converted 3,000 new souls for Christ to replace those lost in a clan fight he felt he could have prevented.

I was privileged to celebrate Holy Communion at the Anglican Bishop's House and Chapel from the Scottish Prayer Book. This deepened our feelings of God's presence in this holy place. My son, John, remarked how safe and not at all alone he felt on Iona. "You could ask anyone for help," he said, "and you would be kindly treated." We met the Rev. and Mrs. Pratt of Kent. They met each other on Iona 25 years ago and have been coming back ever since. Mr. and Mrs. Barnett come every year now. They used to come only every other year, but then the years in between "didn't go so well."

As Iona faded from view on the ferry ride back to Mull, we promised ourselves to try to return and accept Warden Penny Rooms' invitation to stay at Bishop's House and be chaplain while we were there. Iona truly is a special place of God!

*Born December 3, 1916*
*Devoted Priest, Poet, Husband, Father, Grandfather, Friend to All*

# JOHN KIMBALL SAVILLE, JR.

You taught us from the day that we were born
About God's love by every word and deed;
Showing best gifts are not ones we can buy
But those that last and fill our every need.
Truth, patience and concern for all but self,
Respect and reverence for all the earth,
To stay in touch with family and friends,
And see each person's God inspired worth.
We thank you for your steady, quiet faith;
We thank you for your kindness and your care;
We thank you for your courage and your joy;
That we have tried to emulate and share.
In this book are many saints to meet,
By adding you it now is all complete.

*This sonnet was written and included without
the author's knowledge, by his son, John Kimball
Saville III, on behalf of the family and all who
know and love "Father Kim."*

*Hymn 293 "I Sing a Song of the Saints of God"*

# BIBLIOGRAPHY

*Lesser Feasts and Fasts* ©2001, The Church Pension Fund

*Saints Galore* by David Veal. Forward Movement Publications ©1996 Third Edition

*Hymnal 1982* ©1995 The Church Pension Fund

PICTURES
http://santucket.com/lectionary
http://www2.evansville.edu/ecoleweb

*Saints, Signs and Symbols* ©1974 N. Ellwood Post Morehouse Barlow Co., Wilton, Connecticut

*The Illustrated Bible and Church Handbook* ©1966 edited by Stanley J. Stuber, Galahad Books, New York City

*St. Joseph Daily Missal* ©1959 Catholic Book Publishing Co., New York

# INDEX

## A

                                              *page number*

*Aelred*   JAN 12                                  38
*Advent*                                          *192*
*Agnes*   JAN 21                                   45
*Aidan*   AUG 31                                   155
*Alban*   JUNE 22                                  *118*
*Alcuin*   MAY 20                                  *100*
*Alfred the Great*   OCT 26                        *188*
*All Faithful Departed*   NOV 2                     7
*All Saints*   NOV 1                                6
*Alphege*   APRIL 19                               *89*
*Ambrose*   DEC 7                                  *28*
*St. Andrew*   NOV 30                              22
*Andrewes, Lancelot*   SEPT 26                     *171*
*Anne & Joachim*   JULY 26                         *133*
*Annunciation, The*   MARCH 25                     *77*
*Anselm*   APRIL 21                                *90*
*Anskar*   FEB 3                                   *54*
*Antony*   JAN 17                                  *40*
*Aquinas, Thomas*   JAN 28                         *51*
*Ascension*                                        202
*Athanasius*   MAY 2                               *95*
*Augustine of Canterbury*   MAY 26                 *103*
*Augustine of Hippo*   AUG 28                      *154*

## B

*Barnabas the Apostle*   JUNE 11                   *112*
*St. Bartholomew*   AUG 24                         *151*
*Basil the Great*   JUNE 14                        *114*
*Becket, Thomas*   DEC 29                          34
*Bede, The Venerable*   MAY 25                     *102*
*Benedict of Nursia*   JULY 11                     *123*
*Bernard*   AUG 20                                 *150*
*Bloomer, Amelia*   JULY 20                        *127*

*Bonhoeffer, Dietrich*   APRIL 9      *86*
*Boniface*   JUNE 5      *109*
*Book of Common Prayer, First*   JUNE      *108*
*Bray, Thomas*   FEB 15      *59*
*Breck, James Lloyd*   APRIL 2      *82*
*Brent, Charles Henry*   MARCH 25      *78*
*Brigid*   FEB 1      *52*
*Brooks, Phillips*   JAN 23      *47*
*Butler, Joseph*   JUNE 16      *116*

## C

*Catherine of Siena*   APRIL 29      *93*
*Chad*   MARCH 2      *65*
*Christmas Day*   DEC 25      *193*
*Clare of Assisi*   AUG 11      *144*
*Clement of Alexandria*   DEC 5      *26*
*Clement*   NOV 23      *19*
*Columba*   JUNE 9      *110*
*Constance & Companions*   SEPT 9      *159*
*Confession of Saint Peter*   JAN 18      *41*
*Conversion of Saint Paul*   JAN 25      *48*
*Cornelius*   FEB 4      *55*
*Cranmer, Thomas*   OCT 16      *183*
*Crummel, Alexander*   SEPT 10      *160*
*Cuthbert*   MARCH 20      *73*
*Cyril and Methodius*   FEB 14      *58*
*Cyril of Jerusalem*   MARCH 18      *71*
*Cyprian*   SEPT 13      *162*

## D

*Daniels, Jonathan Myrick*   AUG 14      *147*
*David*   MARCH 1      *64*
*De Koven, James*   MARCH 22      *75*
*Dominic*   AUG 8      *142*

*Donne, John*  MARCH  31          *80*
*DuBose, William Porcher*  AUG 18        *149*
*Dunstan*  MAY 19          *99*

## E

*Easter Day*          *201*
*Edmund*  NOV 20          *18*
*Edward the Confessor*  OCT 13        *179*
*Elizabeth*  NOV 19          *17*
*Emery, Julia Chester*  JAN 9        *36*
*Enmegahbowh*  JUNE 12        *113*
*Ephrem of Edessa*  JUNE 10        *111*
*The Epiphany*  JAN 6        *194*

## F

*Fabian*  JAN 20          *44*
*Ferrar, Nicholas*  DEC 1        *23*
*Francis of Assisi*  OCT 4        *175*

## G

*Gallaudet, Thomas*  AUG 27        *153*
*God the Father*          *3*
*Good Friday, The Trial*        *198*
*Good Friday, The Crucifixion*        *199*
*Gregory the Great*  MARCH 12        *69*
*Gregory of Nazianzus*  MAY 9        *98*
*Gregory of Nyssa*  MARCH 9        *68*
*Gregory the Illuminator*  MARCH 23        *76*
*Grosseteste, Robert*  OCT 9        *177*

## H

*Hannington, James*  OCT 29        *190*
*Herbert, George*  FEB 27        *63*

*Hilary*   JAN 13                                                   *39*
*Hilda*   NOV 18                                                    *16*
*Hildegard of Bingen*   SEPT 17                                    *165*
*Hobart, John Henry*   SEPT 12                                     *161*
*Holy Cross Day,*   SEPT 14                                        *163*
*Holy Innocents,*   DEC 28                                          *33*
*Holy Name*   JAN 1                                                 *35*
*Holy Saturday*                                                    *200*
*Holy Spirit*                                                        *5*
*Hooker, Richard*   NOV 3                                            *8*
*Hugh*   NOV 17                                                     *15*
*Huntington, James Otis Sargent*   NOV 25                           *20*
*Huntington, William Reed*   JULY 27                               *134*

I

*Ignatius of Antioch*   OCT 17                                     *184*
*Ignatius of Loyola*   JULY 31                                     *137*
*Independence Day*   JULY 4                                        *122*
*Irenaeus*   JUNE 28                                               *120*

J

*St. James*   JULY 25                                              *132*
*St. James, St. Philip &*   MAY 1                                   *94*
*James of Jerusalem*   OCT 23                                      *187*
*Jerome*   SEPT 30                                                 *173*
*Jesus Christ*                                                       *4*
*Joachim & Anne*   JULY 26                                         *133*
*St. John*   DEC 27                                                 *32*
*John the Baptist, Nativity of*   JUNE 24                          *119*
*John Chrysostom*   JAN 27                                          *50*
*John of Damascus*   DEC 4                                          *25*
*Jones, Absalom*   FEB 13                                           *57*
*Jones, Paul*   SEPT 4                                             *158*

*Joseph*  MARCH 19     *72*
*Joseph of Arimathaea*  AUG 1     *138*
*St. Jude, St. Simon &*  OCT 28     *189*
*Julian of Norwich, Dame*  MAY 8     *97*
*Justin*  JUNE 1     *105*

K

*Kamehameha & Emma*  NOV 28     *21*
*Keble, John*  MARCH 29     *79*
*Kemper, Jackson*  MAY 24     *101*
*Ken, Thomas*  MARCH 21     *74*
*King, Martin Luther, Jr.*  APRIL 4     *84*

L

*Latimer, Hugh*  OCT 16     *182*
*Laud, William*  JAN 10     *37*
*Law, William*  APRIL 10     *87*
*Laurence*  AUG 10     *143*
*Lent*     *195*
*Leo the Great*  NOV 10     *10*
*Louis, King of France*  AUG 25     *152*
*Lucy*  DEC 13     *29*
*St. Luke*  OCT 18     *185*
*Luther, Martin*  FEB 18     *60*

M

*Macrina*  JULY 19     *125*
*Margaret*  NOV 16     *14*
*St. Mark*  APRIL 25     *92*
*Martin*  NOV 11     *11*
*Martyn, Henry*  OCT 19     *186*
*Martyrs of Japan*  FEB 5     *56*

*Martyrs of Lyons*   JUNE 2       *106*

*Martyrs of New Guinea*   SEPT 2       *157*

*Martyrs of Uganda*   JUNE 3       *107*

*St. Mary the Virgin*   AUG 15       *148*

*St. Mary Magdalene*   JULY 22       *130*

*Mary & Martha of Bethany*   JULY 29       *135*

*St. Matthew*   SEPT 21       *169*

*Matthias*   FEB 24       *62*

*Maundy Thursday*       *197*

*Maurice, Frederick Denison*   APRIL 1       *81*

*Methodius, Cyril &*   FEB 14       *58*

*St. Michael & All Angels,*   SEPT. 29       *172*

*Mizeki, Bernard*   JUNE 18       *117*

*Monnica*   MAY 4       *96*

*Muhlenberg, William Augustus*   APRIL 8       *85*

## N

*Neale, John Mason*   AUG 7       *141*

*Nicholas*   DEC 6       *27*

*Nightingale, Florence*   AUG 12       *145*

*Ninian*   SEPT 16       *164*

## O

*Oakerhater, David Pendleton*   SEPT 1       *156*

*Oswald*   AUG 5       *139*

## P

*Palm Sunday*       *196*

*Parents of BVM (Anne & Joachim)* JULY 26   *133*

*Patrick*   MARCH 17       *70*

*Patteson, John Coleridge*   SEPT 20       *168*

*Pentecost*    *203*

*St. Peter & St. Paul*   JUNE 29    *121*

*Perpetua & Her Companions*   MARCH 7    *67*

*St. Philip & St. James*   MAY 1    *94*

*Philip, Deacon & Evangelist*   OCT 11    *178*

*Polycarp*   FEB 23    *61*

*The Presentation*   FEB 2    *53*

*Pusey, Edward Bouverie*   SEPT 18    *166*

# R

*Remigius*   OCT 1    *174*

*Richard of Chichester*   APRIL 3    *83*

*Ridley, Nicholas*   OCT 16    *182*

# S

*Schereschewsky, Samuel Isaac Joseph*   OCT 14   *180*

*Seabury, Samuel*   NOV 14    *13*

*Sebastian*   JAN 20    *43*

*Selwyn, George Augustus*   APRIL 11    *88*

*Sergius*   SEPT 25    *170*

*Simeon, Charles*   NOV 12    *12*

*St. Simon & St. Jude*   OCT 28    *189*

*Stanton, Elizabeth Cady*   JULY 20    *126*

*St. Stephen*   DEC 26    *31*

*Style, Henry Winter*   AUG 27    *153*

# T

*Taylor, Jeremy*   AUG 13    *146*

*Teresa of Avila*   OCT 15    *181*

*Thanksgiving*    *204*

*Theodore of Tarsus*   SEPT 19    *167*

*St. Thomas*   DEC 21                             *30*

*Thomas á Kempis*   JULY 24                        *131*

*Timothy and Titus*   JAN 26                       *49*

*The Transfiguration*   AUG 6                      *140*

*Truth, Sojourner*   JULY 20                       *128*

*Tubman, Harriet Ross*   JULY 20                   *129*

*Tyndale, William*   OCT 6                         *176*


U


*Underhill, Evelyn*   JUNE 15                      *115*


V


*Vincent*   JAN 22                                 *46*

*Visitation, The*   MAY 31                         *104*


W


*Wesley, John & Charles*   MARCH 3                 *66*

*White, William*   JULY 17                         *124*

*Wilberforce, William*   JULY 30                   *136*

*Williams, Channing Moore*   DEC 2                 *24*

*Willibrord*   NOV 7                               *9*

*Wulfstan*   JAN 19                                *42*